CONTENTS

About the authors   v

Introduction   vi

Acknowledgements   vii

1   The role of placements   1

■ How placements are selected ■ What you will gain from
your placements ■ What the placements gain from having
students

2   Types of placement   11

■ Care at home ■ School-based placements ■ Full-time day
care ■ Sessional provision ■ Out-of-school care ■ Hospitals

3   The preliminary visit   27

■ Preparing for placement ■ The first visit ■ The local
environment ■ The role of the supervisor

4   Settling in   37

■ A family placement ■ Group care ■ Registration of Settings
■ Policies and procedures ■ The daily routine ■ Things to do
when there is nothing to do ■ Difficulty in settling in

5   Coursework while on placement   55

■ Observations ■ Keeping a diary ■ Activities and routines
■ The role of the supervisor

6   Communication   68

■ Communicating with adults ■ Communicating with babies
and young children ■ Reading to children

7   Play and learning   82

■ The Early Years Foundation Stage curriculum ■ The National
Curriculum ■ Planning activities ■ Working with babies
■ The role of the student

8   Health and safety   98

■ Safety in the placement ■ Personal health and hygiene
■ Children with HIV (Human Immunodeficiency Virus)

9   Providing food and drink   110

■ A healthy diet ■ Feeding babies ■ Special diets ■ Emotional
and cultural influences ■ Food hygiene ■ Mealtimes

10 Understanding children's behaviour   125

■ Factors that influence behaviour ■ Common types of
challenging behaviour ■ Growing independence
■ Managing unwanted behaviour

11 Child protection   135

■ Definitions ■ Recognition ■ Procedures ■ Professional
behaviour ■ Helping children to protect themselves

12 Parents in placement   147

■ Parents in placement ■ Different family types ■ Various
child-rearing practices ■ Naming systems

13 Succeeding in placement   157

■ Professionalism ■ Anti-bias practice ■ Assessment in
placement ■ Stress in the placement ■ Leaving your placement

Resources   172

Index   175

Notes   180

ABOUT THE AUTHORS

Christine Hobart and Jill Frankel come from a background of health visiting and nursery education. They worked together in Camden before meeting again at City and Islington College. They have worked together for many years, training students to work with young children and have written 12 books encompassing all areas of the child-care curriculum. Christine is an external examiner for CACHE.

Miranda Walker has worked with children from birth to 16 years in a range of settings, including her own day nursery and out-of-school clubs. She has inspected nursery provision for Ofsted, and worked at East Devon College as an Early Years and Playwork lecturer and NVQ assessor and internal verifier. She is a regular contributor to industry magazines and an established author.

INTRODUCTION

In the experience of the authors, there are no basic guides offering help to child-care students working with children from birth to 16 years on how to achieve success in training placements and work experience. New students often do not understand what is expected of them. Despite detailed preparation by college tutors, the practical work, routines of the placement and the expectations of supervisors often prove daunting. In our view, the more knowledge and information that students can obtain the more readily they can settle into a professional team, enabling them to contribute sooner to the work, gaining skills and competences quickly.

This book is designed to be user friendly, describing certain aspects of each type of placement so that students can easily understand the structure and routines of where they are placed. We have created a chart to show most types of placements, detailing staff ratios and qualifications, age range of the children, cost of child-care, inspection arrangements, the curriculum, hours of work and the number of weeks the various placements are open. It would be impossible to cover every single placement so we have left room for students to enter any variation they find in their particular placement.

The theory of child-care and education will be taught by tutors in centres and covered by other texts. We have concentrated on the everyday skills students will need and how to apply these skills in a practical way.

Most chapters will contain the following features:
- Check lists
- Charts
- Case studies
- Good practice
- Activities.

We have used the female gender for the child throughout the book as this is less confusing than changing gender every chapter.

ACKNOWLEDGEMENTS

The authors and publishers would like to thank the following people and organisations:

1 Angela Dare and Margaret O'Donovan for permission to use the chart on page 111.
2 West Thames College tutors and supervisors for permission to adapt the handout on pages 51–53.
3 Suzanne Pye and Susie Sainsbury, Voice for the Child in Care, Chris Satterthwaite, Leslie Frankel, and the Margaret McMillan Centre for permission to use the photographs produced in the book.
4 Cynthia Isaac, Anne O'Brien and Ruth Jno Baptiste for reading the manuscript.
5 The Controller of HMSO and the Queen's Printer for Scotland for permission to reproduce Crown © copyright material under Class Licence No. C01 W 0000195.

Every effort has been made to contact copyright holders, and we apologise if any have been overlooked.

The authors would also like to thank the students they have taught over the years and the training supervisors who ensured their success.

1 THE ROLE OF PLACEMENTS

This chapter covers:
- How placements are selected
- What you will gain from your placements
- What the placements gain from having students

As a student on a child-care and education course you will be spending some of your time in a variety of establishments, working with groups of children from the age of 0–16 years.

If you are on a course leading to a professional qualification, the training placement forms an integral part of the course; and you will be unable to gain the qualification if you are deemed unsatisfactory in your practical work. If you are on one of the introductory courses, such as the

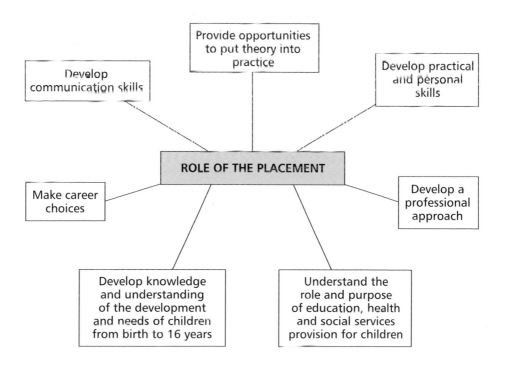

Provide opportunities to put theory into practice

Develop communication skills

Develop practical and personal skills

ROLE OF THE PLACEMENT

Make career choices

Develop a professional approach

Develop knowledge and understanding of the development and needs of children from birth to 16 years

Understand the role and purpose of education, health and social services provision for children

CFCC or GCSE Child Development course, you will spend less time in placement and the time spent will be considered work experience rather than professional training.

It is most important that you understand fully what is expected of you in a placement, and that placement supervisors realize the potential and limitations of each of their students. It is through misunderstandings at the very beginning of a training placement that difficulties and problems arise.

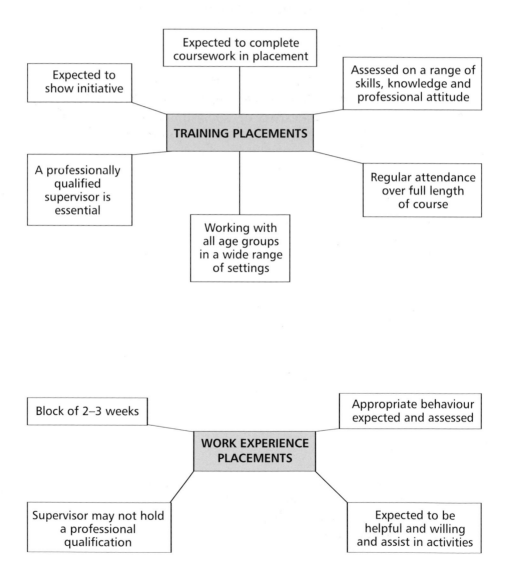

CASE STUDY

Sharon was delighted to be placed in a Nursery School close to where she lived. The school had an excellent reputation and Sharon considered herself lucky to be placed there. She failed to mention to her tutor that her own three children had all attended the school.

When her tutor visited and asked her supervisor how Sharon was progressing, she was horrified to be told that Sharon was doing very well as she knew all the staff and most of the families at the school. Sharon had helped out as a volunteer now and again for several years. Sharon's tutor immediately arranged an alternative placement, much to Sharon's distress.

1 Why do you think the tutor made this decision?
2 List the disadvantages of working in a placement where you have had previous contact
3 How could the misunderstanding have been avoided?

How placements are selected

Your centre will have gone to great lengths to place you in a suitable local establishment. Not every place where there are children will provide the necessary training you need.

REGISTRATION, INSPECTION AND INSURANCE COVER

All group placements must be registered with Ofsted under the Children Act, 1989. This indicates minimal acceptable standards. Placements will hold a registration certificate and will be inspected regularly by Ofsted. Tutors will have access to the latest reports. Without registration, the placement would have difficulty in acquiring insurance cover. The centre must insure students for any time spent in placement.

THE ENVIRONMENT

The placement should be welcoming, warm, safe and clean. All Health and Safety legislation should be fully implemented. All policies and procedures, as discussed in chapter 4, should be in place and available for tutors and students to look at.

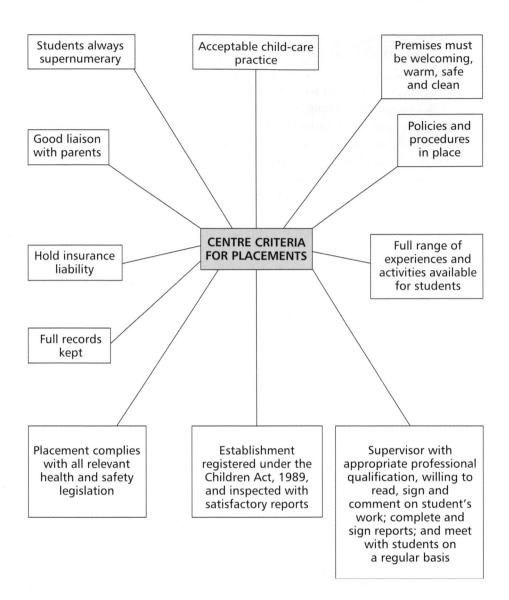

Students always supernumerary

Acceptable child-care practice

Premises must be welcoming, warm, safe and clean

Good liaison with parents

Policies and procedures in place

Hold insurance liability

CENTRE CRITERIA FOR PLACEMENTS

Full range of experiences and activities available for students

Full records kept

Placement complies with all relevant health and safety legislation

Establishment registered under the Children Act, 1989, and inspected with satisfactory reports

Supervisor with appropriate professional qualification, willing to read, sign and comment on student's work; complete and sign reports; and meet with students on a regular basis

THE CURRICULUM

In September 2008, a curriculum known as *The Early Years Foundation Stage* (EYFS) was introduced. It applies to children from birth to the end of the academic year in which the child has their fifth birthday. The EYFS is mandatory for all schools and all early years providers in Ofsted registered settings, including childminders. Settings will plan activities and routines to promote six areas of learning: personal, social and emotional development; communication, language and literacy; problem solving, reasoning and numeracy; knowledge and understanding of the world; creative development; and physical development.

The National Curriculum is taught in primary and secondary schools, from Key Stage 1 to Key Stage 4. Subjects taught include English, Maths, Science, History, Geography and IT.

You may have a placement within a group setting where no curriculum is followed, for instance, in an out-of-school club that caters for older children. But planned activities will still take place alongside other routines, so there will be plenty of opportunities for you to participate in a wide range of care, play and educational activities.

AGREEMENT BETWEEN THE CENTRE AND THE PLACEMENT

Many centres will draw up a contract with the placement, making sure that:
- the named supervisor holds appropriate qualifications and has a commitment to training
- you are given time to observe and assess children
- you are given time to prepare, plan and carry out activities required for coursework
- you are inducted into the policies and procedures of the placement during a preliminary visit or during the first week
- supervisors will endeavour to attend meetings at the centre
- the placement will agree to visits from tutors by arrangement
- you will not be counted as a member of staff, and should never be left in sole charge of any child or group of children.

What you will gain from your placements

During your time in placement you will discover what it is like to be with groups of children of different ages, from various backgrounds and perhaps with some who have a learning, behavioural or physical disability. You will be helping to prepare activities before the children arrive, observing the children, helping to clear up and display their work when they have left for home, evaluating in writing what has happened during the day and then planning for the next day.

The first few days will help you decide if this is the career for you. In fact, many centres insist on students completing a one- to two-week work experience placement, working with a group of children, before offering them a place on a professional course. Completing the chart on page 6 will help you identify your strengths and weaknesses and perhaps show you where you might need to make progress.

Self-assessment before training placement		
Personality profile	**Yes**	**No**
Do you have:		
an outgoing personality		
a sense of humour		
a quiet/calm approach		
perseverance		
knowledge of various cultures		
commitment to anti-discrimination?		
Are you:		
flexible		
sensitive		
assertive		
reliable and punctual?		
Have you had experience working with young children?		
Do you have a range of hobbies and interests?		
Do you have physical stamina?		
Do you relate well to children?		
Are you able to stimulate children to learn?		
Do children feel safe and secure with you?		
Do you feel comfortable working alongside adults?		
Can you accept constructive criticism?		
Do you enjoy:		
creative arts		
sports		
music?		

PRACTICAL SKILLS

Child-care and education practitioners are expected to develop practical skills such as:

■ providing food and drink and preparing meals and snacks
■ making sure that children have opportunities for exercise and being aware that they need to rest when tired
■ keeping hair and skin clean, understanding care of the teeth and feet
■ toilet-training and thus helping children to become more independent and aware of hygiene routines

- avoiding confrontations with children, always reinforcing positive behaviour and responding appropriately to challenging behaviour
- responding to accidents and emergencies and using their knowledge of first aid
- showing awareness of risks and hazards when planning activities
- promoting health routines, for example with regard to road safety and food
- responding with warmth and sensitivity to children who are unhappy.

A family placement with a nanny or child-minder will provide more opportunities than group care to learn about a larger variety of practical skills, such as bathing and sleep routines.

Activity

List some opportunities you might have in caring for children in a family setting that you would not find in group care.

SELF-DEVELOPMENT

Child-care and education courses, more than many other courses, will help you to mature and develop in a variety of ways. The following diagram shows you how you can expect to gain in confidence as you proceed through the course. This is possible because you will be acquiring knowledge in your academic work and applying it immediately in practice.

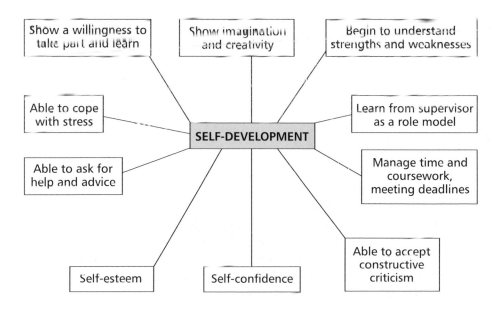

COMMUNICATION

You will be mixing with many adults and children throughout the day, so your ability to communicate will improve rapidly – you will need to understand quickly what is being asked of you and to respond appropriately.

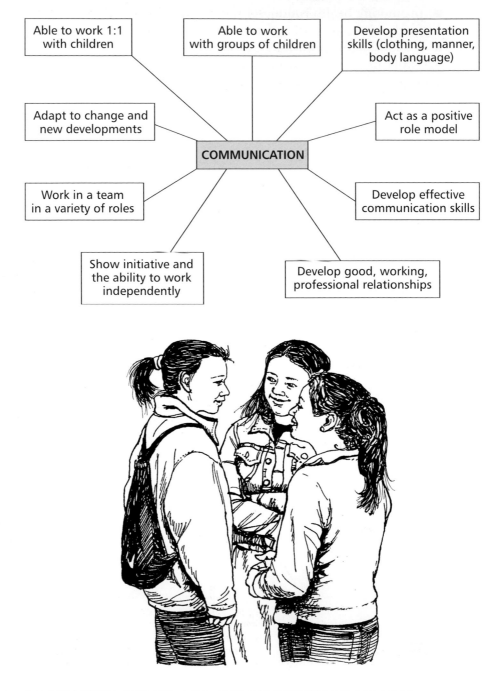

Able to work 1:1 with children

Able to work with groups of children

Develop presentation skills (clothing, manner, body language)

Adapt to change and new developments

COMMUNICATION

Act as a positive role model

Work in a team in a variety of roles

Develop effective communication skills

Show initiative and the ability to work independently

Develop good, working, professional relationships

Jonathan, a mature student, was a great success in his first placement, except for one thing: his tendency to speak very loudly to colleagues and children. This became so irritating that the placement supervisor, after several attempts to get Jonathan to modulate his speech, contacted the centre for help. Jonathan seemed to have no idea how loudly he was speaking.

1 Why is it important not to shout when working with children?
2 Do you think there might have been a physical explanation for Jonathan's loud voice?
3 What other explanations might there be?
4 How might Jonathan be helped?

PROFESSIONALISM

The qualification you receive at the end of the course will give you a licence to practice with very young children in a variety of settings. Each placement allows you to demonstrate that you have an understanding of professionalism.

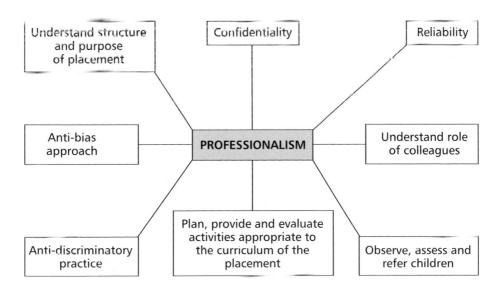

What the placements gain from having students

Placements would not continue to accept students, year after year, if they did not gain something from them. Some of the reasons for having students are to:

- gain fresh ideas for activities, books and music
- make use of a student's particular skill, such as speaking another language or playing a musical instrument
- have another adult who is able to relate on a one-to-one basis with a child who really needs special attention, where the class teacher or child-care and education practitioner might find it hard to find the time
- gain additional observation skills – the student may well pick up on something previously overlooked
- help keep up-to-date, by forging or strengthening links with the local college or secondary school
- ensure a professional commitment to training the next generation of child-care and education workers
- assist in the self-development of the supervisor
- provide an extra pair of hands – this is always welcome, although the placement knows that the student is always supernumerary and so must never be left alone with the children.

You will have the opportunity to try out ideas in your placement, with the permission of your supervisor, which might be difficult to do once you start work. You will enjoy some placements more than others, and this may help you to know which age group and type of establishment you will want to work in once you are qualified.

2 TYPES OF PLACEMENT

This chapter covers:
- Care at home
- School-based placements
- Full-time day care
- Sessional provision
- Out-of-school care
- Hospitals

The following diagram shows all the child-care and education provision available.

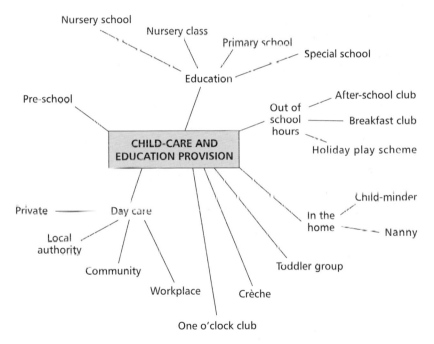

The chart on pages 12–13 outlines the similarities and differences of the various types of establishments and home settings in which you might be placed.

Although we have made the chart as comprehensive as we can, no doubt there will be some variety in the placements that you personally experience. If we took every single placement into account, the chart would take up most of the book!

Range of placements

Types of child care	Age Range	Hours Open	Curriculum	Staff Qualifications	Staffing ratios	Weeks open	Inspection	Cost	Notes on your placement
Care at home Child-minders	from 6 weeks	flexible care	0–5 Early Years Foundation Stage	pre-registration course CCP qualification First Aid 'Fit' person	1 adult to 6 ch. under 8; of these no more than 3 must be under 5; of these 3 no more than 1 under 1 year	50	Ofsted	hourly rate negotiated with parent	
Nannies	from birth	by contract with family	to meet care & developmental needs of children in family	some are qualified to Level 3, some have experience, some have neither	None laid down	n/a	none	£150–£450 p.w. Varies according to qualifications, exp. no. in family, live in/out	
Nursery schools State	3–4:11	5 hours + 1hr dinner p/t 2½ hrs	0–5 Early Years Foundation Stage	qualified nursery teachers working with Level 3 child-care practitioners	2:20	36	Ofsted	free	
Private	2–4:11	f/t 5 hrs p/t 2½ hrs	0–5 Early Years Foundation Stage	as above but could be some variation	2:20 but more if under 2s present	33–36	Ofsted	fees vary depending on hours, area and popularity	
Nursery classes	3–4:11	as above	0–5 Early Years Foundation Stage	qualified nursery teachers working with Level 3 child-care practitioners	2:20	36	Ofsted	free	

	Age	Hours	Curriculum	Staff qualifications	Ratio	Weeks	Inspection	Cost
Infant schools State	4–7:11	6½ hrs inc. brks	National Curriculum	qualified teacher & classroom assistant	2:30	36	Ofsted	free
Private	4–7:11	vary but similar to above	most follow National Curriculum; but can be some additions	as above	2:30	36	Independent Schools Inspectorate	as private nursery schools
Special schools	4+	6½ hrs inc. brks	National Curriculum	qualified teachers child-care practitioners plus range of specialists	varied depending on type of disability	36	Ofsted	free
Full day care including private & local authority day nurseries, pre-schools, children's centres, family centres, workplace nurseries & community nurseries	6 weeks–4:11	varies but generally 7 am to 6 pm	0–5 Early Years Foundation Stage	person in charge Level 3 + 2 yrs experience 50% staff hold Level 2	under 2s 1:3, 2–3s 1:4, 3–7s 1:8	50	Ofsted	free local authority, some free places, most others £100–£200 p.w.
Sessional day care Pre-schools (playgroups)	2–4:11	less than 4 hrs per day	0–5 Early Years Foundation Stage	as above	as above	most follow school terms	Ofsted	£3–£5 per session
Crèches	varies	as above	provision of resources appropriate to age	as above	as above	varies	Ofsted	varies, hourly rate
Out-of-school care including Breakfast Clubs, After School Clubs, Summer Camps, holiday play-schemes	4+	varies	safe care offering play opportunities and range of sports & creative activities with peers. If four year olds are cared for, the EYFS will apply to them	as above	3–7 yrs 1:8	term time or school holidays	Ofsted	£5–£9 for each session; holiday schemes £40–£90; private £150 p.w.

Care at home

Children may be looked after in their own homes or in other people's homes by:

- their family (mothers, fathers, aunts, grandparents)
- nannies
- registered child-minders.

Nannies may be qualified or unqualified, experienced or inexperienced. A nanny may live in the family home or care for the children on a daily basis. They may look after children from more than one family. Qualified nannies often have sole charge of the children, whilst the parents are at work. Nannies are not registered with the local authority or Ofsted. You are unlikely to be placed in a family setting where the nanny is not qualified. Your centre may look for placements where the mother has some relevant professional qualification, such as health visitor, nurse or teacher.

Child-minders are people who look after other people's children in their own home. They have to be registered as a person suitable to care for young children. This involves being checked as to health and character. A criminal-record check will be carried out to make sure they have not committed an offence involving children. Child-minders are inspected annually to make sure standards are maintained. There is now a recognized qualification for child-minders.

Centres will often use home placements in areas of the country where there is no day-care provision for babies and toddlers. It is a course require-

ment for you to have experience of these age groups. When you have worked in a family placement for two weeks, use the following checklist.

CHECKLIST FOR WORKING IN A FAMILY SETTING

Have you:
- assisted with all aspects of physical care
- cared for a sick child
- initiated new play activities for the children
- helped to supervise children's rest, exercise and sleep
- researched and discussed appropriate toys and equipment with the child-minder, parent or nanny
- prepared and cleared away children's meals
- cleaned the children's bedrooms
- done the children's laundry
- accompanied children on leisure activities
- visited the GP or health clinic with the children
- kept up with your observations
- helped to deliver the EYFS (if working with a child-minder)?

If you are working with a baby or babies, complete the following checklist after two weeks.

CHECKLIST FOR WORKING WITH BABIES

Have you helped:
- prepare and give a bottle feed
- sterilize feeding equipment
- change a nappy
- settle a baby for a sleep
- read a story and sing songs to a baby
- in the weaning process
- yourself, by keeping up with your observations?

School-based placements

These might be private or state maintained establishments.

NURSERY SCHOOLS

These are usually attended by children between 2:6 and 5 years old, and staffed by a Head Teacher, nursery teachers, and child-care and education practitioners. The children may stay for the whole day, which usually runs between 9.00 am and 3.00 pm, or for either the morning or afternoon. There should be one member of staff for every ten children. During their time at the school, the children will be encouraged to become independent people by developing physically, intellectually, emotionally and socially. Some schools may put more emphasis on intellectual and language development.

NURSERY CLASSES

These usually have the same aims as a nursery school. Children may attend part- or full-time. There may be fewer staff, usually just one nursery teacher and one child-care and education practitioner for every 20 children. The nursery will be part of the primary school and will join in many of the school's activities, such as assemblies and end of term parties.

The nursery teacher is in charge of the team in which the child-care and education practitioner plays a most valuable role. The child-care and education practitioner will be expected to be responsible for the care and health of the children and to take part in the teaching. It is to him or her that children will often turn if they are unhappy or have an accident. In a good team, all the staff will work together to achieve the best for the children. The various members of the team will have different responsibilities.

CHECKLIST FOR WORKING WITH TWO TO FIVE YEAR OLDS

Have you done the following:
- prepared any creative activities
- read or told a story to a group of children
- led a music session
- cooked with the children
- initiated any outside play activities
- added anything to the Home Corner display
- taken part in any imaginary play
- set up any activities with natural materials
- helped with the preparations involved in celebrating a festival
- been on any outings or visits with the children and staff
- become involved in team discussions, contributing your own suggestions
- taken part in the assessment of any children
- kept up-to-date with your observations
- planned and carried out activities linked to the EYFS
- supported children's learning in the EYFS, within all six areas of learning?

PRIMARY SCHOOLS

In this country, children are legally required to begin attending school the term after they become five years of age. Many children start school before this, sometimes as much as a year early. There are two reasons for this: a

shortage of nursery places; and increased government funding for the number of full-time pupils on the school roll.

No two schools are alike – they may have different beliefs and aims for the children in their care. Some will lay emphasis on academic ability; others may have a good reputation for music, sport or art. Some schools may give a great deal of pastoral care to the families, whilst others may feel this role to be inappropriate for teachers. All state schools will have to carry out the demands of the National Curriculum, which serves to test children's ability in many areas before they move on to junior or middle schools at seven plus.

CHECKLIST FOR WORKING IN PRIMARY SCHOOLS

Have you:
- prepared any creative activities, and seen them finished
- read or told a story with a group of children
- led a music session, perhaps with movement as well
- shopped and cooked with the children
- taken part in curriculum planning
- been on any outings or visits with the children
- become involved in team discussions, contributing your own suggestions
- taken part in helping children with their reading, writing, science and mathematics
- kept up with your observations?

INDEPENDENT SCHOOLS

Some parents will decide to send their children to independent, fee-paying schools. The decision may be made because class sizes tend to be smaller and there is often more emphasis on academic achievement. Some schools offer a particular ethos. For example, the Rudolph Steiner schools follow a particular philosophy, the Montessori schools yet another. At Summerhill, the children are given the freedom to choose their own curriculum. Independent schools are not obliged to follow the National Curriculum, although most of them do abide by most of it whilst also including additional subjects.

WORKING WITH DISABLED CHILDREN

In the past, students and practitioners rarely had the opportunity to work with disabled children unless they did a placement in a specialist setting, such as a special school or an opportunity playgroup. Thankfully, times have changed, and inclusion is now firmly embedded in the ethos of all types of settings. Early Years providers, schools and play settings are legally required to do all that is 'reasonably practical' to meet the needs of disabled children and their families. This may include making physical changes to premises (such as installing a ramp for wheelchair users), adapting activities to make them accessible to all, and providing extra staff support.

Children may have:

■ learning difficulties
■ communication difficulties
■ hearing impairment
■ visual impairment
■ physical impairment
■ emotional and behavioural difficulties.

While some families feel strongly that their child's needs should be met in mainstream settings, other families may prefer their child to attend a specialist setting. Some children have profound and complex needs (which may include medical care), and professionals and the family may feel these needs are best met in a specialist setting. While you should find that you will be working with disabled children in several of your placements, many tutors will still arrange for students to do a placement in a specialist setting.

If you have not worked with disabled children before, you may feel apprehensive. But there's no need to be anxious. The staff will have introduced students with little or no experience to working with disabled children many times. They will be happy to explain things, to answer your queries and to offer reassurance. Often, students who feel nervous about such a placement at first settle down within a couple of days and really enjoy the work. Many go on to decide this is what they want to do when they're qualified. To help you to settle into a specialist setting, spend time observing the routines and understanding how procedures are carried out. Watch the following in particular:

■ How staff communicate with the children.
■ How staff manage a group of children.
■ How staff handle children's behaviour.
■ How children who are incontinent are cared for.
■ How children are lifted/physically supported.
■ Use of special equipment or resources.
■ How medical conditions such as epilepsy are managed.
■ Mealtimes.

Many outside professionals may visit a specialist setting (such as speech and language therapists, physiotherapists, occupational therapists or educational psychologists). This is an opportunity to develop an understanding of each profession and learn how to liaise effectively those involved with the child and their family.

You will find that some settings and families use the term 'special needs' or 'special educational needs', while others use the term 'disabled'. Pay attention to the language used by the staff in each setting, and take your lead from them.

CHECKLIST FOR WORKING WITH CHILDREN WITH SPECIAL NEEDS

Have you:
- supported children of different ages with a range of special needs
- worked with children in both a mainstream and specialist setting
- assisted in the preparation of play and learning
- supported children in their play and learning
- planned and provided your own play and learning activities
- helped to care for children's physical needs by toileting, dressing and assisting them at mealtimes
- taken part in sharing information with a child's family
- participated in physical play sessions/physical education
- observed outside professionals working with children
- read the health and safety policy?

Full-time day care

Full-time day care may be provided by the private or public sector. In a day-care centre, some of the staff will be qualified child-care and education practitioners and others may be experienced staff with little formal training. Other staff may have social-work qualifications, counselling diplomas or other qualifications. As the day is longer, the staff will work shifts, covering the day from 7.30 am to 6.00 pm throughout the year. Holiday time is shorter and the hours may be longer but the salary can be higher than in a school, the opportunities for promotion are much better, and the responsibilities often greater. During your training you would be expected to work six hours a day and, in order to see how the full day functions, you would also be expected to work one or two late or early shifts.

Because of the long hours, children will be allocated a key worker from the staff team. The key worker will liaise with the child's parents and have special responsibility for attending to the child's needs. They will often complete individual observations of the child.

Recently, many more private nurseries have opened. There are now over 70 nursery chains. A chain is made up of private nurseries, owned by one company, which will be similar to each other in the quality of care

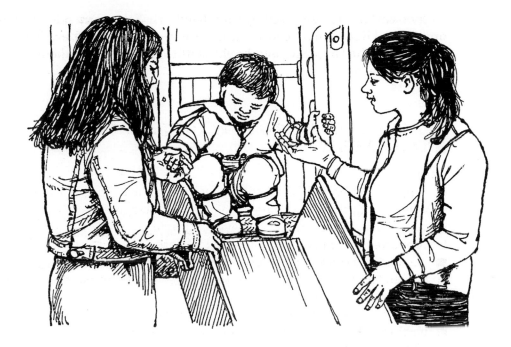

they provide. Some chains have up to 40 nurseries plus holiday play-schemes. Chains may be planning to expand rapidly. Parents' fees are set to cover costs and make a profit for the nursery.

Workplace nurseries might be run by:

■ large institutions such as hospitals and universities for their staff and students
■ businesses such as banks, manufacturing and television companies for their staff
■ a private company.

The nurseries are provided to assist companies in keeping valued and well-trained staff. They will have many young babies, as often the mothers return to work after maternity leave. With more women continuing to work whilst their children are very young, there is an ever increasing demand for places. The hours of workplace nurseries can be very long if necessary – hospital hours may have to be covered for instance, and some university courses run in the evenings.

The number of places for children in local authority day-care centres will vary from area to area. Sure Start is the Government's programme to deliver the best start in life for every child by bringing together early education, child-care, health and family support. Some Sure Start initiatives apply universally, while others only apply in targeted local areas and/or to disadvantaged groups in England.

Responsibility for Sure Start lies with The Early Years, Extended Schools and Special Needs Group, which belongs to the Department for Children, Schools and Families. Sure Start tells us the following about their service:

Services

- Sure Start covers children from conception through to age 14, and up to age 16 for those with special educational needs and disabilities. It also aims to help parents and communities across the country.
- There are a wide range of services currently available, from Children's Centres and early support programmes to information and advice on health and financial matters. We are helping set and maintain child-care standards.
- Sure Start is the cornerstone of the Government's drive to tackle child poverty and social exclusion working with parents-to-be, parents/carers and children to promote the physical, intellectual and social development of babies and young children so that they can flourish at home and when they get to school.
- All Sure Start local programmes have become children's centres. Local authorities are responsible for Sure Start children's centres, and the services on offer may vary from area to area.

How do our services work?

Our services bring together universal, free, early education and more and better child-care. Sure Start does this with greater support where there is greater need through children's tax credit, children's centres and Sure Start local programmes.

Integrated Early Years services

For some time we have been encouraging the delivery of child-care alongside early education and other health and family services.

Sure Start Children's Centres

Sure Start Children's Centres are building on existing successful initiatives like Sure Start local programmes, Neighbourhood Nurseries and Early Excellence Centres, and bringing high-quality integrated Early Years services to the heart of communities.

Our target of 2,500 children's centres was reached in early March 2008, and 2,914 centres have now been established (October 2008), offering services to over 2.3 million young children and their families.

By 2010, the number of children's centres will increase to 3,500 – so every family has easy access to high-quality integrated services in their community and the benefits of Sure Start can be felt nationwide.

Early education

All three and four year olds are now guaranteed a free, part-time ($12\frac{1}{2}$ hours per week, 38 weeks per year, increasing to 15 hours per week in 2010), early-education place. There are over 37,000 settings delivering free, Government-funded, early education in the maintained, private, voluntary and independent sectors.

Child-care

In June 2008, the stock of registered child-care stood at approaching 1.3 million places (more than double the 1997 level).

There will be a child-care place for all children aged between 3 and 14, between the hours of 8.00 am and 6.00 pm each weekday by 2010, when there will be over 2 million sustainable child-care places for children up to 14.

CHECKLIST FOR WORKING IN FULL-TIME DAY CARE

Have you:
- seen the beginning and end of the day, by working in shifts
- seen and understood the role of the key worker
- understood the dietary needs of the children
- helped to supervise meal and snack times
- planned and provided activities to extend all-round development and promote the EYFS
- played a part in toilet-training, in liaison with parents and other staff
- talked and listened to all the children in the group
- comforted a child
- helped a new child to settle in
- read stories to a small group
- attended staff meetings
- understood the role of all the staff in the placement
- helped on outings
- kept up with your observations?

Sessional provision

PRE-SCHOOLS (PLAYGROUPS)

Some pre-schools offer full-time day care but others only open part-time – for three days a week or only in the mornings for instance. Most open school hours during term time only. The parent chooses how often the child will attend; it could be every morning, one or two mornings a week, or both morning and afternoon sessions every day.

The parents are generally involved in the running of the group, both in the day-to-day activities and the management. Most pre-schools were started by parents because there was not enough provision for young children in the area. Although, originally, pre-schools were started mainly for children to learn to socialise and play together, nowadays they offer the full Early Years Foundation Stage curriculum.

A pre-school is often held in a building shared by other groups in the community. This means that at the end of each session each user of the hall has to clear away all the equipment, and this can be quite difficult for the staff.

CRÈCHES

Crèches are places were young children are cared for whilst their parents do other activities, generally in the same building or in local areas. For example, leisure centres, shopping centres and hospitals often provide this facility. Children usually go for a short while and different children will attend each day.

Out-of-school care

Out-of-school settings combine child-care with a safe place to play for children of school age, outside of school hours. This includes before school, after school and school holiday provision. Weekend provision is less common but is offered by some settings. Out-of-school care may be run by the private, public or voluntary sector.

Breakfast clubs usually open at 8.00 am. Staff give children breakfast and look after them until it's time to escort them to school. After school clubs collect children from school, usually staying open until 6.00 pm. Holiday clubs often open all day from 8.00 am to 6.00 pm. Clubs may be attached to another setting such as a school, day nursery or leisure centre.

Typical out-of-school activities include free-play with a wide range of equipment, sport, playground games, art and craft, table-top games and outings during the holidays.

As you will see from the chart on page 25, there are many reasons why parents choose a particular type of child-care provision.

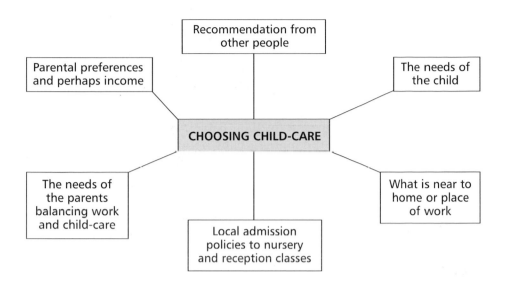

Recommendation from other people

Parental preferences and perhaps income

The needs of the child

CHOOSING CHILD-CARE

The needs of the parents balancing work and child-care

Local admission policies to nursery and reception classes

What is near to home or place of work

THE LIBRARY
NORTH WEST KENT COLLEGE
DERING WAY, GRAVESEND

Hospitals

Some colleges are able to place students in hospitals, either to work with mothers and newly born babies or in paediatric units. It is unfortunate that there are decreasing numbers of opportunities for you to have this experience, due to the other training commitments of the hospital.

You would spend the majority of your time on the obstetric wards, helping mothers to care for their babies. It is valuable experience as you are there to help the mother–baby bonding and to aid in the development of the mother's parenting skills, such as the bathing, day-to-day care and feeding of the baby.

Some time might be spent in the Special Care Baby Unit, with more vulnerable babies. This would be an interesting experience as you must work closely with the midwives in providing intensive care. You might also play a part in helping parents come to terms with the situation and to relate to their babies. You should not be expected to take blood, tube-feed babies or undertake any procedure for which you are not trained.

You might spend time on paediatric wards working with a child on a one-to-one basis or with small groups in a child-centred activity room. Most of the children will be in hospital for a very short time. Some children may be terminally ill and you may find this distressing. A sympathetic nature can help parents and children to deal with the situation.

All your placements will be unique, and different from other students. The range of placements that students will experience will obviously vary greatly from centre to centre and region to region. So you should take every opportunity to discuss your placements with other students in your group.

THE PRELIMINARY VISIT

This chapter covers:
- **Preparing for placement**
- **The first visit**
- **The local environment**
- **The role of the supervisor**

The centre chooses placements because they offer you the opportunity to work where there is good practice and experienced, qualified staff. It would be very unusual for you to be allowed to select your own placement.

Preparing for placement

Before you start any placement, your tutor/placement officer will give you full details including the address, telephone number and names of your supervisor and the organizer/head teacher. In many centres, you may visit the placement before you start. Your centre may arrange this or you may be expected to contact the placement yourself. It will be up to you to find the most convenient and quickest route from your home to the placement. It is worthwhile taking some time to prepare yourself for your first visit.

APPEARANCE

Your appearance should be neat, and you must be careful with your personal hygiene. Your hair should be tidy, your nails short and well cared for, your clothing non-restricting, and your shoes flat and comfortable so that you are able to take a full part in the children's day. Unsuitable clothes, for example, would include high heels and smart clothes that you are afraid of getting dirty. On the other hand, torn or very shabby clothing is equally inappropriate. In some areas, jeans are considered unacceptable wear in schools. Also, visible body piercings would be unacceptable in most placements as children may pull them and cause injury.

Most nurseries ask students to wear inside shoes or slippers when on placement in the baby room for hygiene reasons – babies spend a lot of their time on the floor and it is important to keep the carpet clean.

Out-of-school clubs may ask for trainers to be worn outside so students can participate fully in more adventurous activities.

CASE STUDY

Jennifer takes pride in her extremely long nails. She spends a great deal of time polishing them and wears large rings to show them off. She visits the placement for the first time and is upset when the supervisor tells her that it is not a good idea to have such long nails when working with young children.

1 Why are long nails unsuitable when working with children?
2 What action should Jennifer take?

People often remember their first impression of you, and it is on this that further judgements may be based. If you feel very nervous, try some relaxation exercises, take some deep breaths and start your visit with a smile on your face and a cheerful and eager expression. Be sensitive to the atmosphere in the room, and aware that supervisors may have many demands on their time and attention.

With thought and preparation, you can show your supervisor right from the start that you are a well-organized and reliable person. You will then stand a very good chance of success. Arrive a little before the expected time, and seek out the organizer/head teacher to let him/her know that you are in the building. Take with you some personal information, such as your past experience with children, other qualifications and interests, and the name of your next of kin to contact in any emergency. Your centre may give you a form similar to the one opposite.

Whenever going into a placement, take with you a pen and a small notebook so that you can write down any information you are given, including the details of any events or activities you may be involved in.

The first visit

Because of the shortage of good training placements in some areas of the country, it is possible that you may be placed with a family for your first placement.

Student information for placement
Name Address   Telephone No. (home)   (mobile)

Next of kin
   Name
   Address
 	
Telephone No.

Age of student
Prior experience working with children
Relevant qualifications (e.g. First Aid Cert.)
Interests and hobbies
Any other relevant information

This form may be photocopied for student use. © Nelson Thornes

A FAMILY PLACEMENT

Your centre may arrange for you to meet the family before starting the placement. This is advantageous to you both, as many questions can be asked and points cleared up. You will need to know:

- the names and ages of the children
- times to start and finish, and how flexible the family wish you to be
- whether a meal will be provided or you will be expected to bring your own lunch
- who pays for fares and any admission charges on any visits made with the family
- if there is a garden, so that you can think about outside activities
- the general routine of the day
- if anyone else will be in the house, apart from the primary carer
- if you will get a break
- if there are any pets
- if the family has public liability cover on their household insurance policy.

The family need to know:

- your age
- where you live, so that they can inform you about public transport

- your telephone number, in case they need to contact you
- whether you smoke
- if you have any special dietary needs
- whether you have any allergies
- if you have any experience with young children
- if you have any particular talents, such as playing the piano
- whether you enjoy sports
- if you have any health problems that might prevent you from taking a full part in sharing the care of the children, such as a weak back.

GROUP CARE

Although you will have made an appointment, the supervisor may be busy with the children when you arrive. Be prepared to sit down with a small group of children and quietly enter into any activity they may be doing, until such time as the supervisor is free. Introduce yourself clearly, and listen carefully to any information that your supervisor gives you.

Activity
What was your first impression of the placement? Write down a few notes and check if you had changed your mind by the time you completed the placement.

WHAT TO LOOK FOR DURING THE VISIT

In addition to confirming the names, address and telephone number given to you by your centre, you will spend most of the visit gathering essential information about the placement.

The following checklist shows all the information you will need to get from your supervisor.

CHECKLIST FOR MEETING WITH SUPERVISOR

- What time do I need to arrive in the morning?
- What time can I expect to leave in the afternoon?
- What room will I be working in?
- What breaks will I have?
- Will I have to pay for any meals?
- Is there a booklet about the placement that I can take away and study?
- As a student, will I have access to the policies and procedures of the placement?
- How large is the staff team, and what are the names of the other staff members?
- Is it possible for someone to give me a tour of the building?
- How many children are there in the room in which I will be working? How many are boys and how many are girls?
- Do the children attend part-time or full-time – or some of each?
- Do any of the children have any health or diet needs of which I should be aware?
- What are the cultural backgrounds of the children?
- How many different languages do they speak?
- Is there a dress code for staff?

Some centres may give you a form similar to the one on page 33.

Have a look at the building in which you will be working. It may be purpose-built or converted from an old house. The room may be spacious or rather cramped. The outside play area may have grass, flowers and trees or it may be a rectangle with a hard surface and no planted area at all. Check if the children are allowed to play outside whenever they want to.

The local environment

When you leave, take some time to walk around the area. See what sort of homes most of the children live in. They might be living in blocks of flats or in houses with gardens. There may be shops and markets nearby. The placement might be rather isolated or there could be parks, a community centre and easy access to public transport.

Contract agreed during the preliminary visit

Students on the full-time Diploma and Certificate in Child-care and Education courses are expected to attend placements during normal placement hours, up to six hours a day, excluding lunch and other breaks.

It is helpful during this session to agree the following

Days to be worked _____

Hours agreed _____

Break entitlement _____

Procedure if sick _____

Procedure if late _____

Dress code _____

Arrangements for supervision _____

Other requests from supervisor or student_____

Student's signature

Supervisor's signature

Date

Placement name

You will find that the mix of the children, suitability of the building and pleasantness or otherwise of the environment in which the children live may well have a bearing on their behaviour and their ability to concentrate when in placement. A large airy room and a beautiful garden with grass and trees will make for a calm atmosphere among staff and children. An interesting and exciting environment will lend itself to many outings and visits within the community.

As you walk around, note whether the placement is:
- in an area of high unemployment
- in an isolated position
- surrounded by mainly flats or houses
- near shops
- accessible to public transport
- near a library
- close to a leisure centre
- near a market
- in easy reach of a park
- near a playground.

Using this information and that from the checklist completed with your supervisor, fill in the chart on page 35.

The role of the supervisor

When you arrive at your placement, one of the staff will have been appointed as your supervisor. He or she will be an experienced and qualified member of staff, who will:
- act as a role model
- show you round the placement
- introduce you to the children and the staff team
- explain the policies and procedures of the placement
- be knowledgeable about current child-care and education practice
- outline what you will be expected to contribute
- encourage you to participate in the daily routines
- listen to you, and help you with any difficulties you might have
- monitor your progress and keep you informed on how you are performing
- confirm with a signature that any work you have done has been completed by you
- be in touch with your centre and be knowledgeable about the course you are taking
- write your report
- help you to succeed and respect your contribution.

Placement worksheet
Type of establishment
Type of building
Number of children
Ages of children
Aim of provision

Staff
   Number
   Qualifications
   Roles

Support services in regular contact
Any other information you wish to note
Travel arrangements for me to placement with an alternative route

CASE STUDY

Janet goes to see her tutor to complain that her supervisor, Gareth, is unsympathetic and always finding fault with her. On closer questioning, it appears that Janet is often late and appears unhappy in the placement. Janet tells her tutor that her youngest child, Joe aged 14 months, has been badly burnt by pulling a teapot containing boiling tea over himself when in a café. Joe has to attend hospital on a regular basis. Janet has not confided any of this to Gareth, as she finds him rather cold and aloof. He is only three years older than Janet's eldest child.

1 How might the tutor help Janet?
2 Is Janet behaving in a professional way?
3 Should Janet try to confide in Gareth? If so, how should she approach this?
4 Is Gareth carrying out his role as a supervisor successfully?

Your supervisor will not expect perfect practice as you are in the process of learning, and you must try not to feel threatened or distressed if he or she challenges your practice or behaviour. Constructive feedback should always be helpful, as it should include plans to help you to progress. Make sure you discuss anything you feel unhappy about with your supervisor. The supervisor who tells you your good points and fails to tell you where you might do better is not helping you to succeed.

In rare cases, students do not feel altogether comfortable with the placement they have been allocated, and will probably discuss their concerns with their tutor.

CASE STUDY

Nadia came to see her tutor after her preliminary visit to the placement. As a Muslim, she was surprised to find that she had been placed in a Catholic primary school. She asked if there was any possibility of moving to a secular school.

The tutor tried, but found it impossible to alter the placement. She asked Nadia to stay for the moment and see how she got on. Nadia agreed.

1 What difficulties might Nadia have encountered?
2 Do you think there was any other solution?
3 What might Nadia have gained from this experience?

As good training placements are so difficult to find, it is unlikely that the student will be able to change, and most people settle down well after a day or two. On the other hand, if you discover that you know parents or staff at the placement personally, you should make your centre aware of this – it would be more appropriate to place you elsewhere, in this instance, as you might find it difficult to apply the rules of confidentiality.

SETTLING IN

This chapter covers:
- **A family placement**
- **Group care**
- **Care requirements**
- **Policies and procedures**
- **The daily routine**
- **Things to do when there is nothing to do**
- **Difficulty in settling in**

Starting any placement can make you anxious. The preliminary visit should have given you some reassurance and information. All placements are different and you need to start off with an open mind, prepared to ask questions and work hard.

Working with families is different from working in an establishment such as a school or day-care centre. As you usually have only one person to relate to you might initially find being placed in a family quite stressful. For this reason, most centres chose group care for your first placement. This is not always possible, however, and your centre probably feels you are a confident and capable student if they place you in a family as your initial placement.

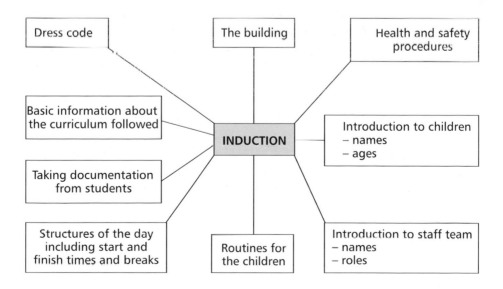

Routines in all placements will vary, and your supervisor will be on hand to induct you into the routines of each particular placement. As soon as possible, hand to your supervisor any documentation, such as time sheets, that have been issued to you by your centre.

A family placement

All families vary in lifestyle, child-rearing practices, ways in which they manage their children's behaviour, diet, routine, bedtimes, religion, cultural background, amount of involvement in play, visits outside the home, watching television, noise levels, pets, housing … the list is endless. They may also vary in their expectations of the skills of the student. Obviously, you have to be flexible and feel confident enough to enjoy the experience of a different way of life. A professional attitude is essential in a family placement. You will need to be punctual, as the children can be disappointed if you do not arrive when expected and, likewise, the parent or carer might feel let down if a planned outing is affected.

CASE STUDY

Julia is an excellent student in her second year. For her family placement she is placed with an Arts tutor from the centre, who is taking six months maternity leave. The tutor has a baby of two months and a toddler of two-and-a-half years.

After the first week, Julia arranges to see her tutor. She is very distressed as the house is dirty and uncared for. There is little food in the house and several items in the fridge are mouldy or beyond their 'use by' date. The family washing has not been done for a full week. The washing-up is continually left from the night before to greet her on her arrival. Bins are overflowing. No one knows when the guinea pig hutch was cleaned out last.

The mother was pleasant and welcoming and the children appeared to be thriving.

1 What help and support should Julia expect from her tutor?
2 Should Julia stay in the placement?
3 How would you respond to this situation?

The following diagrams (pages 39 and 40) show what you might offer the family placement and what the family might offer you.

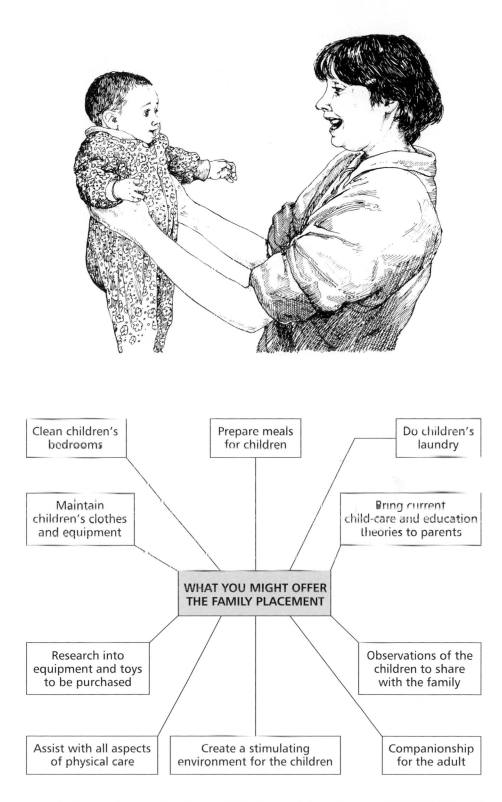

Clean children's
bedrooms

Prepare meals
for children

Do children's
laundry

Maintain
children's clothes
and equipment

Bring current
child-care and education
theories to parents

**WHAT YOU MIGHT OFFER
THE FAMILY PLACEMENT**

Research into
equipment and toys
to be purchased

Observations of the
children to share
with the family

Assist with all aspects
of physical care

Create a stimulating
environment for the children

Companionship
for the adult

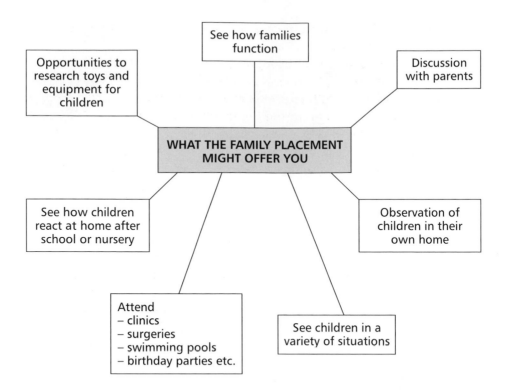

Group care

In most placements where there are groups of children you will be expected to take as full a part as possible in all activities, showing enthusiasm and a willingness to learn. This will help to build good relationships with the staff team. They will see you as a reliable and enthusiastic member of the team and this will be recorded in your final report. Using the following checklist will quickly help you to find your way around the building and settle into the placement.

CHECKLIST

To find your way around, ask the following questions:
- Where are the staff lavatories?
- Where is the staffroom?
- Where can you eat in the building?
- Are you able to buy food in the placement?
- What hours are you expected to work?

You should make sure that the placement knows who to contact should you be unwell or have an accident.

An understanding of how groups work (group dynamics) will help you to settle into your placement. A group is made up of people with individual personalities, different expectations and understanding of their role, and 'hidden agendas' (intentions or ulterior motives which are not necessarily obvious to those around them). Individuals within groups can have a major influence on the behaviour of others, both good and bad. Support and guidance and a sense of group identity may ensure the best possible child-care practice.

CASE STUDY

Ben is a young student, in his first placement. He is placed in a Beacon Nursery School, where the practice is seen to be excellent. The staff team all work together very well, and have developed excellent practice over a number of years. They often go out together on a Friday evening.

Ben feels excluded. The work does not have to be discussed very much as the team all seem to know what they are doing from day to day and week to week. There are many in-jokes and references that are never explained to Ben. When he tried to discuss this with his tutor, she told Ben he was lucky to be training in such a good placement.

1 What steps might Ben take to be included in the planning of the curriculum?
2 How might Ben improve his relationship with the team?
3 Do you think the tutor could do more to help Ben?

Every team member will be focused on what they are trying to achieve within the establishment and what they are expected to contribute. The line management system will be clear, and each member will understand his or her own responsibility and accountability. In a strong team, each member will feel valued and so feel able to express problems knowing that they will be listened to. The whole team will be involved in decision-making, and all the members, including students, will feel their opinions are valued.

GOOD PRACTICE FOR STUDENTS WHEN WORKING IN A TEAM

- Always be willing to help when requested.
- Try to work co-operatively with the whole team, so as not to allow personality clashes or feelings of dislike to interfere with your work.

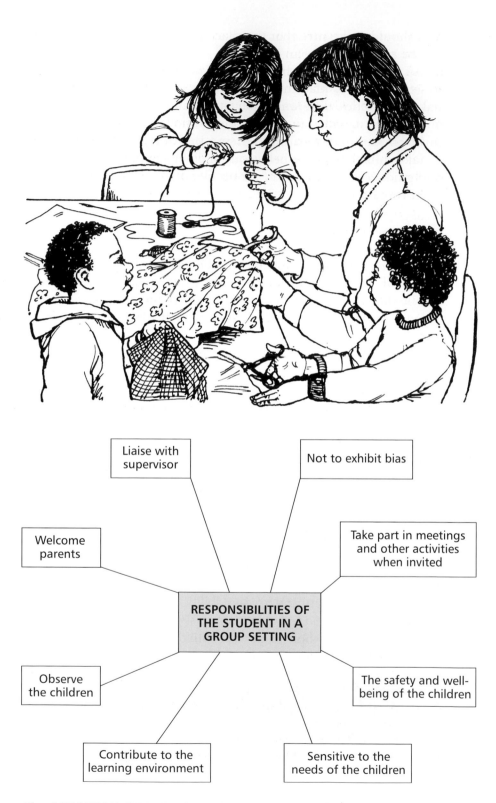

Liaise with supervisor

Not to exhibit bias

Welcome parents

Take part in meetings and other activities when invited

RESPONSIBILITIES OF THE STUDENT IN A GROUP SETTING

Observe the children

The safety and well-being of the children

Contribute to the learning environment

Sensitive to the needs of the children

- Do not overstep the boundaries of the student role. Ask for help and advice when necessary.
- Take direction from staff and accept constructive feedback.
- Respect colleagues' privacy. Do not be inquisitive about other people's private lives. Always keep confidences.
- Do not introduce your own problems into the work setting.
- Be aware of the working environment and respect other people's feelings with regard to temperature, light and noise.
- Never criticize a team member publicly or in their absence.
- Be ready and willing to take part in extra curricular activities whenever possible.
- Try to show initiative.
- Always be reliable and punctual.

You will have met some members of the team at the preliminary visit. You now need to get to know the other members and, of course, the children. Find out how your supervisor and other members like to be addressed while in adult company, and whether this is the same as when in the company of children.

These days, most students are expected to use the staffroom but you should check first that this is so. Some of you might find it a rather uncomfortable place initially. The rest of the team will know each other well and you may feel rather left out of the conversation and ill at ease. It is a good idea to take something in with you like a book or an activity such as sewing.

As you become familiar with the placement you will be included in the general discussion and you will feel more relaxed. Find out if you are expected to pay for tea and coffee, remember to wash up your cup after use and be aware that some staff have their own mugs.

CHECKLIST FOR SETTLING IN

Check to see if you have taken note of the:
- names and roles of each member of the team
- names and ages of the children
- layout of the building and location of essential rooms, such as the staffroom, medical room and lavatories
- routines of the day, week, term and year
- children who have special needs, for example those with speech delay, learning difficulties, or chronic illnesses such as asthma or diabetes
- location of the first aid box, accident book and telephone
- fire drill procedure
- location of the register and record of policies and procedures
- way equipment should be stored, both inside and out.

The more you know about the particular needs of the children in your placement, the better you will be able to contribute to the team. Remember, though, that any information is confidential and should not be discussed with family or friends.

> **Activity**
> Find out from your supervisor whether there are any children in your placement who are being offered special help.

Registration of settings

All day-care providers in England caring for children under the age of eight years are registered and inspected by the Early Years Directorate within the Office for Standards in Education (Ofsted). There are two registers, the *Childcare Register* and the *Early Years Register.*

CHILDCARE REGISTER

This is a register of providers who are registered by Ofsted to care for children from birth to 17 years.

The register has two parts:
- **the voluntary part**
  Providers who are not eligible for compulsory registration may choose to register here. These are mainly people looking after children aged eight and over, or providing care in the child's home (e.g. nannies).
- **the compulsory part**
  Providers must register if they care for one or more children following their fifth birthdays until they reach their eighth birthdays.

Registered settings must meet the **Requirements of the Childcare Register** at all times. Ofsted will carry out periodic inspections of settings to assess the standard of the provision, and will publish a public report which will be available to families using, or wishing to use, the provision. The Requirements fall into the categories below. An example of the content of each category is given here. You can see the requirements in full in the document *The Guide to Registration on the Childcare Register,* available on the Ofsted website (www.ofsted.gov.uk).

Welfare of the children being cared for
Example content of this category:
- *Children receiving child-care are kept safe from harm.*
- *There must be a ratio of one adult to every eight children*

Arrangements for safeguarding children
- *There must be written child protection procedures.*
- *No one unsuitable to work with children has unsupervised access to a child.*

Suitability of persons to care for, or be in regular contact with children
- *There must be effective systems to ensure that those in contact with children are suitable to work with them.*

Qualifications and training
- *At least half of all persons caring for children have successfully completed a relevant qualification at a minimum of level 2.*
- *The manager has a relevant qualification at a minimum of level 3.*

Suitability and safety of premises and equipment
- *Premises and equipment used are safe and suitable for child-care.*

How the child-care provision is organized
- *Where older and younger children are together, the behaviour of children over the age of eight years does not have a negative effect on the younger children.*
- *Child-care is accessible and inclusive by taking all reasonable steps to ensure that the needs of each child are met.*

Procedures for dealing with complaints
- *Each complaint must be fully investigated.*

Records to be kept
- *Certain records must be kept and retained for a period of two years.*

Providing information to parents
- *Information about the activities the children will undertake is given.*
- *Copies of safeguarding procedures and complaints procedures are available.*

Providing information to Ofsted
- *Ofsted must be informed of changes to circumstance as soon as possible.*

Changes to premises and provision
- *Settings must inform Ofsted of a change to the address of the premises where they are providing childcare.*

Changes to people
■ *The registered person must inform Ofsted of a change to their name, address or telephone number.*

Matters affecting the welfare of children
■ *Ofsted must be informed of certain events, including incidents of food poisoning and any serious accidents or injuries to children.*

Insurance
■ *The setting must be covered by insurance for death, injury, public liability, damage or other loss.*

Certificate of registration
■ *The certificate of registration must be displayed.*

All child-care providers must also comply with other relevant legislation including that covering health and safety, disability discrimination, food hygiene, fire and planning requirements.

EARLY YEARS REGISTER

In addition, since 2008, all child-carers providing for children from birth to the 31 August following their fifth birthday must register on the Early Years Register and deliver the Early Years Foundation Stage (EYFS), which is a curriculum framework. You'll read more about this in Chapter 7. Settings delivering the EYFS must meet the EYFS welfare requirements. The welfare requirements fall into the following five categories:

Safeguarding and promoting children's welfare
■ The provider must take necessary steps to safeguard and promote the welfare of children.
■ The provider must promote the good health of the children, take necessary steps to prevent the spread of infection, and take appropriate action when they are ill.
■ Children's behaviour must be managed effectively and in a manner appropriate for their stage of development and particular individual needs.

Suitable people
■ Providers must ensure that adults looking after children, or having unsupervised access to them, are suitable to do so.
■ Adults looking after children must have appropriate qualifications,

training, skills and knowledge.
- Staffing arrangements must be organized to ensure safety and to meet the needs of the children.

Suitable premises, environment and equipment
- Outdoor and indoor spaces, furniture, equipment and toys must be safe and suitable for their purpose.

Organisation
- Providers must plan and organise their systems to ensure that every child receives an enjoyable and challenging learning and development experience that is tailored to meet their individual needs.

Documentation
Providers must maintain records, policies and procedures required for the safe and efficient management of the settings and to meet the needs of the children.

Policies and procedures

Written policies exist to protect children and staff. They make sure that everyone understands the rules and the underpinning ethos of the establishment. Without policies there would be a lack of direction with people working at cross-purposes, perhaps putting children and staff at risk.

Policies which you can expect all settings to have in place include:
- *Accident and emergency* – including evacuation procedures, first aid, use of an accident book and procedures if a child is lost. Written risk assessments are also required.
- *Arrivals and departures* – including registration and collection procedures, and procedures followed if a child is not collected as arranged.
- *Behaviour* – including how inappropriate behaviour is handled.
- *Child protection* – including procedures if child abuse is suspected.
- *Complaints* – including the procedure for parents wishing to complain to Ofsted.
- *Confidentiality* – including how information is stored with regard to the Data Protection Acts.
- *Equal opportunities* – including how an inclusive service is offered.
- *Food and drink* – including how this is provided.
- *Health and safety* – including hygiene procedures to prevent cross infections, risk assessments and illness.
- *Medicines* – including the written permission necessary for administering medication.

Outings – including risk assessment and parental permissions.
Working with parents – how the setting works in partnership with families.

Placements have to comply with employment laws and will have policies and procedures for staff recruitment, contracts of employment, job descriptions, grievances and dismissal.

You should make a point of discussing with your supervisor, whenever you start a new placement, the policies and procedures with which you need to be familiar. Most establishments keep copies of their policies and procedures in the general office and in the staffroom. As you progress on the course, you might be interested to read the policy about staff recruitment.

You need to remember that your placement owns the copyright of the policies and procedures they have written, and you must not pass them on to other establishments.

The daily routine

After a day or two, you will be ready to take part in the general routine of the day, being sensitive to the needs of the placement and of the children.

The following chart shows you the activities that will be included in your day.

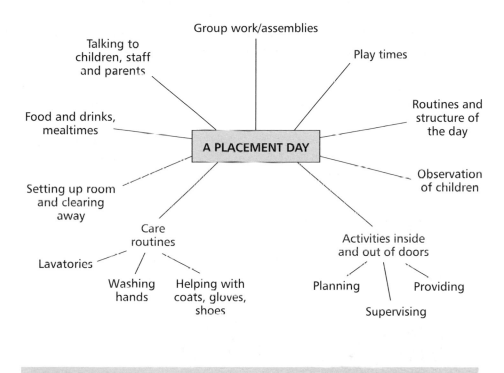

Activity
Using the above chart as a guide, work out how the day is organized in your placement.

Many students find it useful to keep a notebook to write down questions they need to ask, and to record activities in which they have taken part. Arrange with your supervisor a time each week when you can discuss your progress and any difficulties you may have come across. At the end of each day, you will need to find out what is expected of you the following day.

Your placement will have set procedures and policies, such as equal opportunities and health and safety policies. You will need to learn, fairly soon after arrival, the fire drill and the procedures for reporting accidents, dealing with emergencies, collecting and delivering children and settling in.

Taking part in the social life of the placement is very important. Try to arrange to use the staffroom at break times, so that the staff can see that you think of yourself as one of them. You may find it intimidating at first but, with a little effort on your part, you will soon relax and become a full member of the team.

CASE STUDY

Siobhan is placed in an Infant School. She enjoys being with the children but is very shy when she has to talk to adults. She sits in the staffroom away from other people, reading a book and not taking part in any conversation. She hopes no one will notice her or ask her any questions. Her hair falls over her eyes as she sits huddled in her chair.

1 What might Siobhan be thinking about as she sits in the staffroom?
2 Is there any help she can get to overcome this problem?
3 If she finds it so difficult to speak with adults, is she on the right course?
4 How might you help any children who are shy, so that this does not become a lifetime habit?

You should always be punctual, arriving at least half an hour before the children. If you find you might be unavoidably late, make sure you telephone and let the placement know. If you become ill and unable to attend the placement, you must telephone as soon as possible. Then keep in touch, on a daily basis, so that they will know when to expect you back.

You might find that you are very tired at the end of a busy day in the placement. This is to be expected as dealing with groups of young children can be exhausting. As you gain in confidence, you will make good and lasting relationships with children and colleagues, and enjoy every minute of your time there.

CHECKLIST FOR AFTER ONE WEEK IN PLACEMENT

- Are you arriving at the expected time?
- Have you attended every day?
- Have you telephoned if you have been absent or late?
- Do you know the names and ages of most of the children?
- Do the children know your name?
- Do you know the names and the roles of all the staff team?
- Have you used the staffroom?
- Have you enjoyed being with the children, looking forward to every day?
- Do you have a clear understanding of what is expected of you in the placement?
- Have you discussed your placement assignments with your supervisor?

Things to do when there is nothing to do

There may be times when you are unsure what to do, and feel you are just standing around feeling awkward and uncomfortable. The following lists, adapted from a handout prepared by the tutors and supervisors at West Thames College, might give you some ideas.

Foundation level students might:

1 tie up any loose shoe laces
2 wipe any runny noses
3 hang up aprons lying on the floor
4 pick up equipment on the floor
5 take part in outdoor play
6 sharpen pencils
7 put the tops on felt pens
8 tidy books
9 do the washing up
10 read with the children
11 play with the children
12 check the lavatories are flushed
13 check there is soap and towels in the bathroom
14 check there is sufficient lavatory paper
15 tidy up the Home Corner and the dressing-up clothes
16 sweep up any sand on the floor
17 mop the floor around the water tray
18 make sure you know how to play the table-top games

19 prepare fruit for snack time
20 talk to the children
21 feed the pets
22 wash toys and dolls
23 pick coats up from the floor
24 check toys and equipment for safety
25 sort pencils and pens into the right pots
26 check jigsaws for missing pieces
27 water the plants
28 wash the aprons
29 mend the dressing-up clothes
30 check the spare clothes cupboard and tidy
31 get to know the children
32 learn to spell the children's names correctly in the correct format
33 learn correct pronunciation of the children's names
34 make sure you know the policies and procedures of the establishment
35 make sure you know the routines of the establishment
36 learn the names of all the staff
37 cover boards ready for new displays
38 make sure you know the computer games
39 check the cassette tapes with the story books
40 know the fire drill
41 read some of the books in the book corner
42 invent a game for the children to play
43 collect resources for the sand and water areas
44 check the Home Corner – and think of anything else that could be used there
45 clean the tables and chairs
46 sort out lost property
47 clean up easels and paint pots
48 ask staff if there is anything you can do to help them.

Level 2 students might also:
1 participate during singing time
2 stock up paper for drawing/painting/writing area
3 put tracing paper on tracing cards
4 tidy display tables
5 clear paint rack and file paintings
6 check display boards and repair or replace torn paper
7 wash 'play dough' equipment
8 tidy resource area
9 tidy book corner
10 mend torn or broken books

11 empty water tray
12 fill up paint pots
13 fill up glue pots
14 empty juice and milk cartons
15 tidy the washrooms
16 play with children
17 clean out pets
18 tidy cupboards
19 join in PE session
20 cut paper into different shapes and sizes for painting and drawing
21 make finger puppets for rhyme time
22 make rhyme cards
23 wash dressing-up clothes
24 learn new rhymes
25 learn parents' names (correct surnames)
26 familiarize yourself with the use of TV and video equipment
27 check cooking cupboard and utensils
28 clean ingredients cupboard
29 wash soft toys
30 check paints and refill powder paint pots.

Level 3 students might add:
 1 make small books for writing area
 2 set up computer
 3 switch off computer
 4 familiarize yourself with computer programmes
 5 put up displays
 6 make labels for equipment
 7 plan a story session for the following week
 8 do another observation
 9 prepare equipment for the next day
10 prepare activity for the next day
11 check on resources for themes
12 learn roles of all the staff
13 check protective clothing for staff (disposable gloves, aprons)
14 take down old displays
15 check cooking ingredients and throw away those passed their 'sell by' date
16 find or make props for a story
17 check name cards and replace lost, ripped or bent ones.

When working in an establishment, you need to be clear about your role, and accept that you will be working under the direction of others, who will delegate tasks to you. You will come to understand the structure. Instructions are generally given verbally. Listen carefully, and make sure you understand what you are being asked to do. If anything is unclear or ambiguous, you must ask for clarification.

> **Activity**
> Find out who, in your placement, sits on the board of governors or management committee. Whom do they represent? How does this come about?

Difficulty in settling in

Sometimes students feel unhappy in their placements and have difficulty in settling in. If this is true of you, ask yourself the following questions:

- Have you been there long enough to give it a chance?
- Are you sure you would settle in more easily somewhere else; or have you, perhaps, made the wrong decision about working with children being the job for you?
- Are you sure you know what the problem is?
- Have you discussed any problems with your supervisor or just kept them to yourself?
- Do you think too much is being asked of you?
- Do you find there is not enough to do?
- Do you feel very much on your own, and not included in the staff team?

If you cannot find an answer to your anxieties and unhappiness, talk it over with your tutor. If the tutor then feels there are real grounds for you not settling in, he or she may decide to find you another placement.

Whether you are placed in group or family care, it should not take you very long to settle in and enjoy the placement.

5 COURSEWORK WHILE ON PLACEMENT

> **This chapter covers:**
> - **Observations**
> - **Keeping a diary**
> - **Activities and routines**
> - **The role of the supervisor**

All child-care and education courses require aspects of the coursework to be carried out in the placement. Students will be expected to undertake a variety of tasks, such as observing children; keeping diaries; planning, implementing and evaluating activities and routines; providing resources; and carrying out other pieces of work that demonstrate their growing skills, knowledge and competence. This work will result in the production of portfolios to be assessed at the end of the course.

Observations

WHY DO OBSERVATIONS?

Observing children is an important part of child-care and education work. Watching children carefully and objectively is a difficult skill to learn. (If ten people witness a traffic accident, ten different descriptions will be given to the police!) You will need to decide what it is you want to observe, then discuss with the supervisor the aim of the observation, and finally sit down quietly in a corner of the room to make your notes.

Normal development
From recording observations, you will learn about normal child development, integrating theory with practice. You will study normal development so that you will understand what is unusual. It is obviously important to be able to assess children who may be behind in terms of physical, intellectual, social or emotional development, so that the child-care practitioners can help a child, or make a referral for specialist help. It is also important to be aware of the child who is advanced in some areas of development, so that a more stimulating programme can be planned.

Changes in behaviour

There might be a sudden change in the behaviour of a child. Careful observations are useful in this case, as the behaviour might have a physical cause, such as the onset of infection, or it might be an emotional response to family problems.

It is necessary to understand that all children are individuals, so will behave and react differently in similar situations. For example, one child might like to stroke a dog or cat, while another would be too timid to do so; each reaction is valid and you should respect them both. Through close observation, you will be able to predict individual behaviour and reactions to situations.

Identifying good practice

Through observing other professionals meeting the needs of children from many different backgrounds, you learn to identify good practice and become aware of your own role. The placement will benefit from your observations when they come to plan and review their practice.

By recording observations of groups of children – not just individuals – you will see different patterns of behaviour, and the interactions of the individuals within the groups.

Health care and safety
You will learn about health care and safety for all the children and, by careful observation, will become aware of their health needs and the dangers around them. You will also learn to recognize the signs and symptoms of a large range of childhood illnesses.

Children's needs
It is important to understand the needs of children, and to become sensitive and perceptive in meeting these needs. It is only by recording objectively what you see, that you can learn in a practical way to become aware of these needs and how to meet them. It also shows you when the child is ready to move on to the next developmental stage. For example, a child walking by holding on to furniture will soon be ready to use push-and-pull toys.

Students sometimes feel that centres set up obstacles for them to overcome, but doing observations to a high standard is not a hurdle to be jumped but a contribution to a satisfying career. As a child-care and education practitioner, observing children will become second nature to you. You will have developed considerable skills in perception, both visual and aural, and will be able to record information clearly, concisely and accurately.

HOW DO YOU MAKE OBSERVATIONS?

There are many different ways of carrying out observations. In general, the technique that you choose will depend on the type of observation you wish to do. You can observe an individual child or a group of children. Whatever method you employ, you must try to be as objective as possible, and only record what you see.

You need to make yourself as inconspicuous as possible, sitting quietly with a pen and paper in a corner of the room. Your placement will give you time to record your observations in note form, and not expect you to take part in any activities while you are doing this. Make sure all the staff in the room know what you are attempting, so there is less chance of you being interrupted. It is not good practice, generally speaking, to do observations involving yourself, so if the child or children insist on you taking part in what they are doing, give up, and try to observe later in the day. It is easier to start by observing just one child for a short period of time. Try to concentrate just on the child; it is seldom relevant to remark on the behaviour of adults. Detailed descriptions of activities in which the children are involved also have no place in your observation. Pretend you are wearing blinkers – just look at the child!

When you have completed your notes, you should read them through to make sure they make sense and then write them up in your own time. Your supervisor should set aside some time during the week to discuss your observations with you, and to sign them as a true and accurate record.

CASE STUDY

On her first day in placement, Monica decides to record an observation. She observes a group of children playing outside with the supervisor, gets out her pad and pencil and her course notes. She is unsure where to start, as she does not know anything about the children she has decided to observe.

Behind her, a fight starts in the playground among a group of three year olds. Mud is flying in all directions, one of the children slips and bangs her head, while another is shouting abusive remarks.

1 What should Monica have found out before starting the observation?
2 What aim do you think Monica had?
3 With whom should she have discussed her proposed observation?
4 What preparation should Monica have made before starting her observation?
5 How should she respond to the fight?

Keeping a diary

You may not be required to keep a diary, (sometimes known as a log or a daily record), but you may find it a useful aid to your memory. It should be written up at the end of every day in placement to show changes in the daily routine such as outings and medicals. It might record the visits of other professional colleagues, such as therapists, the police and the local child protection team. The diary could show the opportunities you have had for recording observations and assessments of children, as well as the time given to provide, implement and evaluate activities, or to manage challenging or worrying behaviour. It would allow you to evaluate your day, what you might like to change and how this might affect your future planning.

Some centres give their students a chart on which to quickly record information, which they might use to reflect on their practice. The chart on page 60 shows how this might be recorded.

You should inform your supervisor that you are keeping a diary. It must be stored in a safe and secure place to maintain confidentiality.

Activities and routines

Most child-care and education courses will require you to keep a portfolio of the work you have carried out with children of all ages in your placements.

Your supervisor will have been told by your centre what is expected of you, and he or she will have been involved in planning the curriculum for the placement. Once you have settled in, you will begin to understand how to plan, implement and evaluate activities and routines. These may be part of a curriculum plan, a theme or a topic that the placement has chosen in order to promote the children's learning and development.

YOUR PROFESSIONAL ROLE

All work produced in the portfolio must show evidence of your understanding of the professional role. As with your observation file, confidentiality must

Daily practice record			
Date	**Placement**	**Arrival time**	**Departure time**
Observations completed			
Activities carried out			
Resources used			
Observed work of other professionals			
Problems encountered			
How problems were resolved			
Books read to children			
Interaction with children			
Meeting with supervisor			
What I contributed to group time			
Contact with parents			
Outgoings			
New skills			
Other comments			

be maintained. If wishing to use material relating to a particular child, you must ensure anonymity of the child and of the staff team. Do not use photographs of anything that might identify a child, although photographs of displays you have produced or artefacts you have made are acceptable. You need to be sensitive to equality of opportunity and anti-discriminatory practice. Your file should include many pieces of work that demonstrate this. For example, if you found in your placement that boys were excluded from playing with dolls, you might like to set up an activity particularly for the boys, of washing dolls and dolls' clothes. When carrying out a cooking activity, you could choose food and utensils from a variety of cultures, encouraging children to enjoy new tastes.

Safety and the protection of the children is your prime responsibility. All aspects of your work should reflect that you have considered this in your planning, implementation and evaluation. Check the suitability of your proposed activity with your supervisor.

CASE STUDY

Eloise has decided to initiate a clay activity with a group of three year olds in a nursery class. Her supervisor is late arriving and the teacher agrees to the activity. The clay has gone hard, so she decides to soak it in a bucket of water for ten minutes.

She calls the children to the table and talks to them about the properties of the clay while waiting for it to soften. The children become excited and start using the clay, which has now become very soft, slippery and slimy. In a very short time, clay is all over the place, in the children's hair and clothes, on the floor and on the walls. The supervisor arrives and is horrified.

1 Why was the supervisor horrified?
2 Should this activity have taken place at this time?
3 How could all the mess have been prevented?
4 Was the activity a complete failure, or did the children gain from this experience?

GOOD PRACTICE IN PLANNING, IMPLEMENTING AND EVALUATING ACTIVITIES

1 All activities, experiences and equipment should be appropriate to the level of development and ability.
2 Allow ease of access to the activity and the equipment.

3 Mop up spills quickly.
4 Make sure you have adequate supervision of the children at all times.
5 Explain the rules of safety to the children in a way they can understand and regularly reinforce these rules.
6 Carry out standard checks of all equipment and materials before use.
7 Remove defective equipment from use.
8 Comply with health and safety regulations when collecting and disposing of waste consumable materials.

You might be asked to sign a statement verifying that all work presented in the portfolio is yours, undertaken on the date, time and place stated.

CURRICULUM PLANS

Curriculum plans are plans of proposed work with groups of children or with an individual child. The Council for Awards in Children's Care and Education (CACHE) has stated that 'a curriculum plan provides a range of activities and experiences proposed to promote particular areas of learning and learning outcomes appropriate to the development of the child'.

Your tutor will discuss this with you and indicate how many such plans you will be expected to submit. They should cover the total age range and demonstrate an ability to plan various appropriate activities and experiences for the areas of play and development, and the Early Years curriculum.

You will see plans in your placement that have been made on a daily, weekly or fortnightly basis, and some that have been devised for a month, a term or even a year. These will be helpful to you when you are compiling your own plans. As with all your work, anti-discriminatory practice should be at the forefront of your thoughts, and you might need to adapt your plans for children with special learning or sensory needs.

DETAILED ACTIVITY PLANS

From each curriculum plan, you will be expected to implement a number of detailed activity plans. You will need to describe the aim of the plan, the proposed learning goals for the children and for yourself, your role in implementing the activity and an evaluation of the activity. When describing your role you will need to describe in full the part you took in the activity and the reactions and responses of the children, even if it went wrong or simply not as you had anticipated.

In an Early Years setting, you'll be expected to plan and implement detailed activity plans to support the Early Years Foundation Stage. During your infant school placement, you will be expected to plan and implement detailed activity plans to support the learning of children in accordance with the National Curriculum. These should link with the planning that has been undertaken by the Early Years practitioners or the class teacher.

You will need to produce a resource that you have developed or made yourself for some of the detailed activity plans. These might include:

- appropriate play materials
- games
- musical instruments
- books
- audio tapes and CDs
- story props
- sensory materials
- mathematical or science packs
- charts
- display or interest tables.

Your tutors will assess whether your resources are appropriate to the age of the children, relevant to the activity and learning goals, in keeping with anti-discriminatory practice, safe, durable and presentable.

Completing the charts on pages 64 and 65, immediately after your implementation, may help you when you write up your evaluation.

Activities for children 1 to 7 years

EVALUATION OF ACTIVITIES

Activity: _____

What went well?

What went wrong?

Did you meet all the aims of the activity?

Did the activity allow active collaboration and involvement of the children?

What would you change in future plans?

How would you follow up this activity?

How does it link to future activities?

For infant school activities: how did you involve the children in the learning process?

Activities for children 1 to 7 years

MONITORING FOR EQUAL OPPORTUNITIES

Activity:_____

How does the activity encourage collaborative learning at some point in the process?

List the opportunities for the development of language.

How does the structure of the activity provide access for all the children?

How could the activity recognize the validity of all the children's cultures and backgrounds?

How does the activity encourage children to develop social and interpersonal skills?

Routines

CACHE has stated 'that any routine should support the care and development of children'. Routines are systematic events that may occur daily, weekly, termly or annually. They could include those involving the physical care of the child, such as hand washing, nappy changing, mealtimes or opportunities for rest, sleep and play. They could refer to special seasonal events such as a summer outing, festivals such as Christmas, or a birthday party. On the other hand, a routine could be a daily check of outside equipment, the weekly washing of dressing-up clothes, or the termly inspection of buildings for maintenance. They may also include visits to professional settings, such as the clinic or the hospital; or involve other professional colleagues, such as health visitors, librarians or speech therapists. You may present the work in a similar way to a detailed activity plan but you should remember to take account of the social and financial environment of the child and the family where appropriate.

Drawing up plans and routines

In the detailed plan and in routines, you will be expected to give an aim and a reason for these plans, and spell out the learning goals for the children and for yourself. You will be remembering the value to the areas of development that you have already outlined, and expecting to promote and extend learning. You may include examples of children's work if you think it is appropriate.

In your detailed plan or routine, you will need to describe the preparation required for the activity. This will include provision of essential materials, additional materials to enhance the activity, protective equipment and clothing, and some indication of cost. You will have to consider the age of the children, possible involvement of one or more parent or carer, and the timing and the duration of the activity. As with any activity, you should take into account safety and anti-discriminatory practice.

Evaluation

This is perhaps the most important part as, when looking at your completed portfolio, you and your tutor should see evidence of your progress reflected in your practice. The following are some criteria you might use:

1 For yourself: did all go as planned? If not, did it matter? How would you do it differently another time?
2 For the children: what did the children learn? Were the areas of learning promoted and extended as planned? How could you make sure they were promoted and extended another time?
3 Was the activity age-appropriate? How would you make this activity appropriate for a) older children and b) younger children?
4 Did all the children have an equal opportunity to use the materials in

this activity? Were you able to extend the children's understanding of anti-discrimination, and present yourself as a positive role model? Is this activity suitable for children with a sensory or learning impairment? If not, can it be adapted?

5 Did any accident occur? If so, how did you deal with it?

6 Were any parents/carers involved, either in the planning or in the implementation of the activity?

7 Did you choose suitable materials? Did you have enough materials? Did the materials cost more than you had anticipated?

8 Were the children involved in the preparation and the tidying up of the activity? Could you have involved them more?

9 Have you looked critically at the whole process of planning and implementing the activity?

The role of the supervisor

All observations, activities, plans and routines that you undertake need to be discussed in full with your supervisor first. While in no way expecting the supervisor to do your work for you, you nevertheless will have to consider the needs and constraints of the placement regarding timing, types of experience, and the needs of individual children. You will have to fit in with the curriculum devised by the placement and be ready to change your ideas if necessary. The supervisor may be asked to comment on your work and will be expected to authenticate it. Please allow plenty of time for reading, assessing and discussing your work.

6 COMMUNICATION

> **This chapter covers:**
> - **Communicating with adults**
> - **Communicating with babies and young children**
> - **Reading to children**

An ability to communicate well with others in the placement is a vital skill. Communication means speaking and listening to others, and responding to others with gestures and facial expressions (body language). The way you communicate with children is most important. You must never sound patronizing or talk down to children. Babies and toddlers with little or no language will still be aware of how you relate to them by the way you speak to them and carry out physical caring tasks.

Communicating with adults

SPEECH

There is no better way of communicating than talking with people. This helps build relationships better than using memos, faxes or e-mails ever can. Always speak clearly, slowly and with expression, particularly when in formal situations or when the information is important. You will be using speech in informal, day-to-day conversations, with your friends, colleagues and the children. From time to time you will be using speech to give information privately to others; at others times it will be to give information publicly, for example at staff meetings.

The drawback to using speech as a method of communication is that sometimes you have to make a quick reply, with little time to think it through first. Speech is generally not as precise as written language, and it is unlikely that you will keep a copy or record. In replying, be aware of your listener's background, knowledge and feelings, and what your ideas will mean to him or her.

In some placements you may be fortunate to see signing used as a method of communication. This may be used as fluently as speech.

Some people communicate better with speech than in writing but for some it is the other way round. You will need both skills to be an effective child-care and education practitioner.

WRITING

A child-care and education practitioner has to be capable of communicating information, ideas, directions and requests in writing and this will take many different forms.

Schools and nurseries place a great deal of emphasis on clearly written labels on children's work and displays. If labelling is required, the writing should be done in lower case with a capital letter at the beginning. The writing should be clear and well formed. The chart on page 70 should help you with this task.

When writing for your own information – such as a daily diary, a list of things to remember or a note to remind yourself to bring in certain objects for the Home Corner – you can record this information in whichever way is most useful to you.

When writing informally to others in your placement, you might decide to use memoranda (memos). A memo is a short, informal note with a message put across as simply and clearly as possible. It must show:

- who the message is to go to, and copies (cc) to anyone else
- who it is from
- the date
- the subject.

It can be handwritten or typed, mailed or e-mailed. It should be initialled and dated at the bottom. There is a danger that some organisations may

use them instead of speaking directly to colleagues. Too many memos may result in people not bothering to read them properly.

In more formal situations, remember to:

- be clear about why you are writing
- use short sentences, that get across your exact meaning
- check the spelling and the grammar
- keep a copy (preferably use a black pen as this photocopies best)

- be as neat and legible as possible (typing it helps)
- date all correspondence
- stick to the facts and be objective.

ANSWERING THE TELEPHONE

In your placement you may find yourself having to take telephone messages. When recording a telephone message, remember to note:
- who the message is from, and his or her telephone number
- who the message is for
- the date and time the call was received
- the subject of the actual message
- your name, as the taker of the message.

People use different voices on the telephone, and the one you use to chat to your friends may not be suitable at work. As there is often some noise on the line, speak very clearly, a little more slowly than usual, and do not allow your voice to drop ('disappear') at the end of the sentence. Give the name of your placement, your name and role. If taking a message for someone else, repeat the message to make sure you have heard correctly. If making a call, immediately say who you are and where you are from and make sure that you are speaking to the correct person. Be clear about the purpose of your call. Personal calls should not be made from your placement telephone unless there is an emergency.

To	Dawn
Date/Time	04.06.09 10.30 am
From	Judy Crisp 0208 857 1693
Message	Judy will not be able to come in tomorrow as arranged to help in the class. She will see you tomorrow afternoon when she collects Simon.
Taken by	Sheila Smith

Remember always to be polite – you may not be seen but you will be heard.

CASE STUDY

Cheryl is on placement in a busy Nursery School. As she goes into the school office to take in some dinner money, she hears the telephone ringing. After a while, she thinks she should pick it up and take a message. Just then, two boys come into the office and start a fight over a football.

The person on the telephone has a very quiet voice but Cheryl is too shy to ask the caller to repeat himself. The boys distract her, and when she puts the phone down she realizes that she has no idea who has rung, who the caller wanted to speak to and only remembers that the message was urgent.

1 Should she leave the room and forget about the call?
2 Should she dial 1471 and try to find out who called, even if it makes her look silly?
3 Should she confess all to her supervisor?
4 How should she have handled the situation at the time?

LISTENING SKILLS

When working with people it is as important to develop your listening skills as your speech. Being a 'good' listener does not come naturally to everyone. You need to listen carefully to others, concentrate, look interested and not interrupt, and never finish sentences for the speaker. This is especially true when listening to children, who may take longer to put over their ideas than adults. Give them time. Ask questions if you need more information.

Remember that in some circumstances you may not be listening properly. If you are worried or upset about something you may not be able to concentrate. Other noises or movements in the room may distract you.

Listening is a positive activity, therefore the good listener does not relax when listening but has to understand and think about what is being said in order to make an appropriate response. It may be necessary to let the speaker see that you are listening carefully by using sounds such as 'Mmm' and 'Uhuh', which show your interest and understanding.

BODY LANGUAGE

Remember that your body is sending out messages at the same time as you are talking and listening. To be effective, all the messages you are sending, including body language, should be in agreement. Communication is spoilt when body language differs from what is being said. Think about:

- your posture
- eye contact
- facial expression
- energy level
- position of your feet and legs when sitting
- personal space
- touching others.

For example, whilst talking to your supervisor, positive body language would show you looking at him or her, smiling and leaning towards each other. Negative body language would be you yawning, looking or turning away, looking at a clock or watch, going off into a daydream and missing conversational cues.

MEETINGS

Meetings range from the very formal to the informal, and during the time spent at your placement you may go to both. Your colleagues, your supervisor or the noticeboard will tell you about meetings. You will need to find out who goes, what is usually discussed, where and when the meetings are held, how long they last, whether they are formal or informal, and whether or not you are expected to attend.

FORMAL MEETINGS

All meetings are different but there are some things common to all, such as having an agenda, minutes and matters arising, and an opportunity to raise any other business at the end of the meeting. Meetings can be large or small but there will usually be a chairperson and someone to take the minutes (notes of what is said and what is decided).

The agenda of the meeting should be issued in advance as it sets out what is going to be discussed. For the more formal meetings, the agenda has a standard form, which notes apologies for absence, minutes of the last meeting, and matters arising from them. This is then followed by the items to be discussed at the meeting, and finishes with any other business and the date of the next meeting. If the group meets regularly, minutes of the last meeting are sent out with the agenda.

Written minutes should be:
- taken in note form then written up in complete sentences, using the past tense
- brief, but with enough detail to let anyone not at the meeting understand what was discussed, what decisions were made, and what action was decided
- a true record of what took place.

When attending a formal meeting, prepare yourself well by reading the agenda and minutes if they are available. Think what you can add to the meeting, and what you might wish to gain. If you want to speak, wait until there is a pause, and always address the person who is chairing the meeting. You may be nervous the first time you speak in a meeting so remember to:

- be positive
- accept that you will be nervous beforehand and try some relaxation techniques
- concentrate on the task, remembering that you are trying to give a message
- take your time
- speak your words more clearly for a larger audience and if you forget your words, pause, take a breath, remember what you want to say and carry on.

Communicating your thoughts to others – whether in speech, writing or body language – is an essential part of the work of the child-care and education practitioner and you should continually try to improve your performance in these areas. Practice helps, and you should take any opportunity you are offered to become more skilled.

Communicating with babies and young children

Someone who wishes to work with young children needs to be responsive, warm and caring. This will show in the way they hold a baby, dress a toddler or speak and listen to a child.

GOOD PRACTICE WHEN HANDLING BABIES AND YOUNG CHILDREN

1 Approach children calmly and quietly, using your voice to encourage co-operation.
2 Make eye-contact with children before attempting to pick them up.
3 Sit on the floor with young children, if you tower over them they might feel threatened.
4 Changing a baby's nappy, brushing a child's hair, and helping a child to use the lavatory are all intimate activities, and preferably should only be carried out once a good relationship has been established.
5 A young child's need to be cuddled should be met immediately, although some schools might frown on physical contact with older children. A child will feel safe and secure if her needs are met swiftly

and responsively. Refusing to pick up and cuddle a child who obviously wants you to is not only bad practice but can be positively harmful to the development of the child.

6 Understand young children's body language. They do not always have the language to explain how they feel.

Activity

Sit with a friend and brush his or her hair, first roughly, not looking, your thoughts are obviously elsewhere. Then repeat gently. Change places with your friend, and then discuss how you both felt.

SPEECH

An important way of communicating with children is through the use of language. Few children have any memories of the time before they were two years old, as this is the age when they start to put thoughts into words.

CASE STUDY

Colette is a young enthusiastic student who is obviously enjoying her placements. Whenever her tutor visits her, she is surrounded by children all trying to talk at once. Whatever activity she is involved in appears to be the favourite with the children. She has a great fund of stories from her childhood and a repertoire of poems and songs from many different countries.

1 What makes Colette so popular?
2 Could she make better use of her skills?
3 What do you think has made her so confident?
4 In what ways do you think she adapts her stories and songs for the different age groups?

GOOD PRACTICE WHEN SPEAKING TO YOUNG CHILDREN

1 Try not to ask children 'closed' questions where you know the answer (such as what colour are your shoes?) The child will either think you are stupid if you don't know your colours or else will feel that she is being tested.
2 Try not to ask children questions that require just one word as an answer (such as do you like apples?) This sort of question does not extend the children's speech and the talk then becomes dominated by the adult.
3 Some of the activities in the nursery lend themselves to adults and children sitting down together. These times are excellent for making

children feel comfortable and relaxed, so that a conversation can take place. The dough or clay table is one such example, dinner time is another.

4 If you want children to carry out a task you must make sure that you explain it simply and clearly. Asking a child if he would like to help you clear up might justify the answer 'no!' – the child is not being defiant but will respond much better if you just tell her politely to do it.

5 Never ask children to do several things at once.

6 Give children time to work out what they want to say. Young children are less experienced conversationalists than adults, so need time to respond.

7 Build good relationships with those children who do not speak to you straight away. When they trust you sufficiently, they will speak to you.

8 Reading books and telling simple stories, to one or two children at a time, helps to build trusting relationships as well as letting the children hear new words and so extend their vocabulary.

9 Talking to children whilst engaged in a play activity with them helps to widen their vocabulary.

10 Speak softly, calmly and clearly to children.

11 Never correct a young child's speech. Grammatical errors are normal for three and four year olds, and will correct themselves as the child develops. A variety of different dialects are there for us all to enjoy and who is to say which is the 'right' one, just so long as speech can be understood. If a child has difficulty in being understood outside the family, specialist help may be necessary.

12 If a child asks you a question to which you do not know the answer, be honest enough to say so, and discuss ways of discovering the answer together.

13 Remember to use music and rhymes with children. Bilingual children often feel more relaxed singing in a language other than their home language, than they do in direct speech.

14 Try to ignore swearing; and make sure you never use 'bad language' yourself. Children give up swearing if they get no reaction.

15 The language you use clearly shows your attitudes and values. Monitor your own speech, showing respect for all the children in your care. Choose carefully the songs and stories you wish to share with the group.

16 Challenge children and adults who use derogatory terms in everyday conversation with others. Explain clearly why this is not acceptable.

17 Always be positive and polite, avoiding sarcasm or argument with a child.

BILINGUAL CHILDREN

To be fluent in two languages is a great advantage in later life, not least because it may lead to the easier learning of third and fourth languages. Children who do not speak English at home find it natural to learn it as a

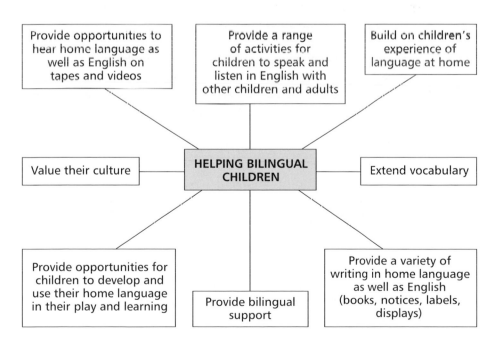

second language in a good nursery, and it is unnecessary to make any special provision for this. Bilingual children (speaking their home language and English), who come to primary school without attending a nursery first, might need additional support. Young children need opportunities to use their home language, so this should be encouraged.

It will take time for you to become automatically sensitive to your language and body contact with children. As you experience how children can be helped to acquire and develop language and other communication skills, you will be able to devise your own activities and ideas to help children with difficulties in communication and language delay, and to extend those children's skills who are already articulate and confident.

Activity

You must discuss this task first with your training supervisor and ask advice and permission to tape a conversation with a child who enjoys a conversation with an adult. Your supervisor may feel it necessary to gain the permission of the child's parent or carer first.

Collect some miniature (small world) toys such as model animals, cars or 'play people'. Then invite the child to sit with you in a quiet corner of the room. Talk with the child about the toys, and see how you can encourage the child to speak. When you have played your tape back:

1   See how much of the speech is yours and how much is the child's. Usually, adults dominate the talk without meaning to and this can be quite revealing.

2   Now look at the quality of the speech. How many 'open' questions did you ask, requiring more from the child than a one-word answer? How many 'closed' questions did you ask, allowing the child to simply answer 'yes' or 'no'? Did the child ask any questions or initiate any ideas?

If you feel that you might do better if you try again, ask permission to do so. It is quite a difficult skill to listen and give the child time to talk, instead of filling in silences with your own chatter!

CHECKLIST

To assess your progress, ask yourself have you:
■   spoken to all the children in the placement every day
■   spent at least ten minutes with a child who is normally reluctant to talk
■   read a story to one child
■   read a story to a small group of children

- told a story to one or more children
- made sure that you have spoken in a soft, clear voice
- spoken clearly when you have asked children to perform tasks
- sung songs with the children
- taught the children a new rhyme
- taken time to discuss displays, posters or interest tables with the children?

CASE STUDY

Josie is placed in an Infant School and is helping to supervise the playground during dinner time. She overhears two six-year-old boys quarrelling. The verbal abuse gets out of hand when one makes a racist remark.

1 What should Josie do immediately?
2 With whom should she discuss this?
3 Should the parents be informed?
4 How might the staff team approach this matter in the classroom?

Reading to children

When in placement you will be expected to read and tell stories to children. At first, you will probably be asked to read to just one or two children who may have nothing particular to do, or who seem upset when their parent has left them at the beginning of the day. You might be asked to read a book that a child has brought with her, which can be a little tricky if it proves to be unsuitable for reading aloud. Try to divert the child with a book you know well, which you feel she will enjoy.

Sit down with the child in a quiet corner of the room, hopefully on a comfortable chair or couch, holding the book so that you can both see the pictures. Let the child dictate the pace at which you read the book. You may not complete the story, as the child might want to comment on the pictures and ask many questions, then suddenly get bored and run off to join in a group activity. If other children want to share the story, ask the child's permission first and, if she minds, promise to read to the other children later.

When you have settled in to your placement, you will be asked to read to a group of children. Many students are apprehensive about this but, like any other activity, preparation is the key. The smaller the group, the more the children will gain. This is particularly true of the younger children.

Make sure the story you choose is:

- appropriate to the age group
- known well and enjoyed by you
- has positive images
- is not frightening in any way.

Your voice should not be dull and monotonous. Try and cultivate different tones and pitches when you are reading dialogue.

Timing is important. Children will not gain a great deal from a story read just before dinner time, when they are hungry, or home time when they are tired. Try to read stories in the middle of 'working' sessions, when children are able to concentrate.

Some books may have many words in them that are unfamiliar to the children. It is not a good idea to change the words as it deprives the children of learning new vocabulary. If the language is so difficult that the children become bored, read it to older children instead, on another occasion.

The importance of communicating well with children and adults cannot be over emphasized. The key to success in your relationships in placement is to make yourself understood and listen carefully to others so that you are aware of the needs of both colleagues and children.

7 PLAY AND LEARNING

This chapter covers:
- **The Early Years Foundation Stage**
- **The National Curriculum**
- **Planning activities**
- **Working with babies**
- **Working with toddlers**
- **The role of the student**

Children's play, also called 'children's work', shows adults what children can understand and do. Play is an essential part of a child's daily life and promotes all-round development. Through play, the child experiences life and learns to understand the world and her place in it. Play develops through several stages:
- Solitary (on her own).
- Parallel (playing alongside another child or adult).
- Associative play (playing with other children).
- Co-operative play, involving planning and games with complicated rules.

When a child attends a registered Early Years setting she will follow the Early Years Foundation Stage. As children enter the infant school, their learning is dictated by the National Curriculum.

The Early Years Foundation Stage curriculum

Since 2008, the Early Years Foundation Stage has been mandatory for:
- all schools
- all Early Years providers in Ofsted registered settings.

It applies to children from birth to the end of the academic year in which the child has their fifth birthday.

In the *Statutory Framework for the Early Years Foundation Stage* the Department for Education and Skills tells us that:

Every child deserves the best possible start in life and support to fulfil their potential. A child's experience in the early years has a major impact on their future life chances. A secure, safe and happy childhood is important in its own right, and it provides the foundation for children to make the most of their abilities and talents as they grow up. When parents choose to use Early Years services they want to know that provision will keep their children safe and help them to thrive. The Early Years Foundation Stage (EYFS) is the framework that provides that assurance. The overarching aim of the EYFS is to help young children achieve the five Every Child Matters outcomes...

Every Child Matters is the Government agenda which focuses on bringing together services to support children and families. It sets out five major outcomes for children:

- Being healthy.
- Staying safe.
- Enjoying and achieving.
- Making a positive contribution.
- Economic well-being.

The EYFS aims to meet the *Every Child Matters* outcomes by:

- **Setting standards** for the learning, development and care young children should experience when they attend a setting outside their family home. Every child should make progress, with no children left behind.
- **Providing equality of opportunity and anti-discriminatory practice.** Ensuring that every child is included and not disadvantaged because of ethnicity, culture, religion, home language, family background, learning difficulties or disabilities, gender or ability.
- **Creating a framework for partnership working between parents and professionals**, and between all the settings that the child attends.
- **Improving quality and consistency in the early years** through standards that apply to all settings. This provides the basis for the inspection and regulation regime carried out by Ofsted.
- **Laying a secure foundation for future learning** through learning and development that is planned around the individual needs and interests of the child. This is informed by the use of on-going observational assessment.

Activity
Visit The Every Child Matters website at www.everychildmatters.gov.uk for further details.

Settings delivering the EYFS must also meet the EYFS welfare requirements.

Themes, principles and commitments

The EYFS is based around four **themes**. Each theme is linked to a **principle**. Each principle is supported by four **commitments**. The commitments describe how their principle can be put into action. The themes, principles and commitments are shown in the table below.

Theme	Principle	Commitments
1. A Unique Child	Every child is a competent learner from birth who can be resilient, capable, confident and self-assured.	1.1 Child development 1.2 Inclusive practice 1.3 Keeping safe 1.4 Health and well-being
2. Positive Relationships	Children learn to be strong and independent from a base of loving and secure relationships with parents and/or a key person.	2.1 Respecting each other 2.2 Parents as partners 2.3 Supporting learning 2.4 Key person
3. Enabling Environment	The environment plays a key role in supporting and extending children's development and learning.	3.1 Observation, assessment and planning 3.2 Supporting every child 3.3 The learning environment 3.4 The wider context
4. Learning and Development	Children develop and learn in different ways and at different rates. All areas of learning and development are equally important and interconnected.	4.1 Play and exploration 4.2 Active learning 4.3 Creativity and critical thinking 4.4 Areas of learning and development

Additional statements are provided within the EYFS to explain each commitment in more detail.

Areas of learning and development

Theme 4, Learning and Development, also contains six *areas of learning and development*:

■ Personal, social and emotional development.
■ Communication, language and literacy.

- Problem solving, reasoning and numeracy.
- Knowledge and understanding of the world.
- Physical development.
- Creative development.

Each area of learning and development is divided up into aspects. You can see these on the Department for Education and Skills Learning and Development card, reproduced below. Together, the six areas of learning and development make up the skills, knowledge and experiences appropriate for babies and children as they grow, learn and develop. Although these are presented as separate areas, it's important to remember that for children everything links and nothing is compartmentalised. All areas of learning and development are connected to one another and are equally important. They are underpinned by the principles of the EYFS. Each area of learning also has a list of early learning goals (elgs). The aim is for children to reach the goals by the end of their Reception year.

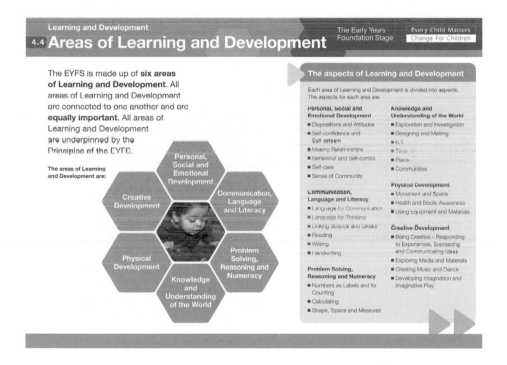

Learning and Development

The Early Years Foundation Stage | Every Child Matters — Change For Children

4.4 Areas of Learning and Development

The EYFS is made up of **six areas of Learning and Development**. All areas of Learning and Development are connected to one another and are **equally important**. All areas of Learning and Development are underpinned by the Principles of the EYFS.

The areas of Learning and Development are:

- Personal, Social and Emotional Development
- Communication, Language and Literacy
- Creative Development
- Problem Solving, Reasoning and Numeracy
- Physical Development
- Knowledge and Understanding of the World

The aspects of Learning and Development

Each area of Learning and Development is divided into aspects. The aspects for each area are:

Personal, Social and Emotional Development
- Dispositions and Attitudes
- Self-confidence and Self-esteem
- Making Relationships
- Behaviour and Self-control
- Self-care
- Sense of Community

Communication, Language and Literacy
- Language for Communication
- Language for Thinking
- Linking Sounds and Letters
- Reading
- Writing
- Handwriting

Problem Solving, Reasoning and Numeracy
- Numbers as Labels and for Counting
- Calculating
- Shape, Space and Measures

Knowledge and Understanding of the World
- Exploration and Investigation
- Designing and Making
- ICT
- Time
- Place
- Communities

Physical Development
- Movement and Space
- Health and Bodily Awareness
- Using Equipment and Materials

Creative Development
- Being Creative – Responding to Experiences, Expressing and Communicating Ideas
- Exploring Media and Materials
- Creating Music and Dance
- Developing Imagination and Imaginative Play

In summary

Child-carers working in settings following the EYFS need to meet the standards for learning, development and care. Their responsibilities include:

- *planning a range of play and learning experiences that promote all of the aspects within all of the areas of learning*

- *assessing and monitoring individual children's progress through observational assessments*
- *using the findings of observational assessments to inform the planning of play and learning experiences*
- *ensuring that children's individual interests and abilities are promoted within the play and learning experiences.*

EYFS resources for childcarers
All settings will have the EYFS pack of resources for providers, which includes:

The Statutory Framework for the Early Years Foundation Stage
This booklet sets out:
- the welfare requirements. You can find out more about the welfare requirements on pages 46–47.
- the learning and development requirements. Which set out providers' duties under each of the six areas of learning and development.

Practice Guidance for the Early Years Foundation Stage
This booklet provides further guidance on:
- legal requirements
- the areas of learning and development
- the EYFS principles
- assessment.

24 cards
Which give the principles and commitments at a glance, with guidance on putting the principles into practice. They include an overview of child development.

CD-ROM
Which contains all the information from the booklets and cards. It includes information on effective practice, research and resources.

The EYFS website is also a valuable resource. Visit www.standards.dcsf.gov.uk/eyfs/.

The National Curriculum

The English National Curriculum (National Curriculum) sets out the minimum curriculum requirements for all maintained schools, including:
- the subjects taught
- the knowledge, skills and understanding required in each subject

- attainment targets in each subject
- how children's progress is assessed and reported.

Within the framework of the National Curriculum, schools are free to plan and organise teaching and learning themselves. Many schools choose to use Schemes of Works from the Qualifications and Curriculum Authority. These help to translate the National Curriculum's objectives into teaching and learning activities for children.

Key stages

The National Curriculum is divided into four **key stages** that children pass through as they move up through the school system. These stages are in addition to the Early Years Foundation Stage described earlier:

- Year 1 and Year 2 of primary school are known as Key Stage 1.
- Years 3 to 6 of primary school are known as Key Stage 2.
- Years 7 to 9 of secondary school are known as Key Stage 3.
- Years 10 to 11 of secondary school are known as Key Stage 4.

Subjects at Key Stage 1 and 2

The compulsory National Curriculum subjects for Key Stages 1 and 2 are:

- English
- mathematics
- science
- design and technology
- information and communication technology (ICT)
- history
- geography
- art and design
- music
- physical education.

Schools also have to teach:

- religious education.

  Parents have the right to withdraw children from the religious education curriculum if they choose.

Schools are advised to teach:

- personal, social and health education (PSHE)
- citizenship
- one or more modern foreign language.

There are **attainment targets** and a **programme of study** for each subject. Programmes of study describe the subject knowledge, skills and understanding pupils are expected to develop during each key stage. It's acceptable for schools to use different names for the subjects, as long as they're covering the National Curriculum.

Mathematics

Mathematics is part of everyone's life. Children need to learn how to estimate, measure, solve problems and handle money. In the infant school children explore mathematics through practical activities and discussion. They learn spatial relationships, quantities and how to solve problems. Much emphasis is placed on mental maths where children develop the ability to add, subtract, divide and multiply in their heads. A numeracy session will be held each day. The mathematics programme of study focuses on:

- number
- shape, space and measure
- handling data (in Key Stage 2).

English

Literacy sessions take place each day. The English programme of study focuses on:

- speaking and listening
- reading
- writing.

Activities children take part in include:

- drama activities
- reading stories
- recognising words from common spelling patterns
- using capital letters, full stops and question marks.

Levels and formal teacher assessments

Attainment targets are split into **levels**.

Teachers carry out regular checks on children's progress in each subject. There will also be **formal teacher assessment** at the end of Key Stages 1–3. (Pupils will usually take GCSE/equivalent exams at the end of Key Stage 4.) This indicates which National Curriculum level best describes individual children's performance in each subject. Schools send parents a report telling them what National Curriculum levels their child has reached in formal assessments.

For more information about the National Curriculum, follow the links at www.direct.gov.uk.

Planning activities

In another book in this series, *A Practical Guide to Activities for Young Children*, we describe how to plan and carry out play and learning activities in detail, showing what equipment you will need, the value to the areas of learning and development, good practice, safety and anti-bias practice and resources. You will be expected to plan, prepare, carry out and evaluate detailed activities in your coursework and this book will prove to be an invaluable aid to your success. If you are working with children aged 4–16 in a play setting (such as an out-of-school club) the book *A Practical Guide to Activities for Older Children* will be extremely helpful. You will learn how to plan a broad range of play activities and themes, how to consult with children and how to promote fun, freedom and flexibility within planned activities.

Working with babies

If no one in your family has had a baby in recent years, you may have little experience and knowledge of how to care for babies and toddlers. This is something that many new parents face too. Remember that you are on placement to learn – if you knew everything already, you wouldn't need to go! And unlike new parents, you won't be expected to care for babies and toddlers alone while you are learning.

Babies begin learning and developing as soon as they are born – many would say from the moment of conception. The neonate quickly learns to recognize the face, smell, feel, taste and voice of the mother, thus using all the senses to ensure survival.

In addition to love, protection, shelter and food, the baby also needs stimulation. At first the mother provides all the stimulation the baby requires, through gentle handling and stroking, speaking in a soft voice, and feeding the baby on demand.

As the baby develops, the interaction between the mother and the baby becomes increasingly important. The baby's routine becomes more established, and there is time to play when feeding, bathing and changing nappies. As the baby begins to spend longer periods of the day awake, so comes the time to truly interact and ensure that the baby is not left alone and bored.

Encouraging development

By six weeks, most babies are smiling, showing that they are responding to a stimulus. This is the time to introduce other stimuli, such as mobiles and rattles. The mobiles that will interest the baby most will have horizontal pictures, so that the baby can gaze at them while lying face upwards. Bright colours add interest, and some have a musical attachment. They can be bought or made at home. Babies also learn by taking all objects to their mouths, so all toys must be carefully checked for safety: they need to be durable, well made, non-toxic, without sharp edges, and be impossible to swallow.

By far the most important stimulus is still consistent contact given to the baby by parents, siblings, grandparents and other familiar adults. Interacting with songs and cuddles and talking to the baby will aid emotional, cognitive and language development. The first response will be facial – smiles and intense looks. Be sure to take turns, and listen to the baby when she begins to vocalise.

After changing the baby's nappy, allow some time for play with hands and feet, unrestricted by clothing. Most babies enjoy their bath times, getting pleasure from the warmth of the water and the freedom to kick and splash.

At three months, the baby discovers her hands and begins to engage in finger play. By six months, this area of hand–eye co-ordination is usually well established and the baby can reach out for a desired object and grasp it. Initially, toys such as activity centres that hang suspended just within the baby's reach will help develop this skill. Playmats with a range of different sensory activities will help stimulate the baby's interest.

Increasingly, the baby's responses are no longer just reflex reactions to sensory stimuli. They become selective, choosing which stimulus to react to. Lightweight rattles and toys that can be easily held in the hand, help to develop hand–eye co-ordination further.

When the baby is able to sit up with support, other toys can be offered. The baby will enjoy knocking down towers built of plastic or foam bricks, banging saucepan lids with a wooden spoon and having fun with weighted or suction toys that stay within the baby's reach.

Singing to a baby comes naturally to most parents. From action songs to finger rhymes, from nursery rhymes to lullabies, the baby will get pleasure from them all, and enjoy a sense of security and comfort. Singing helps babies to discriminate sounds and anticipate repetitive actions.

It is important to read to a small baby as the baby will not only enjoy the close contact but also begin to recognize familiar objects in the picture books. It is a useful introduction to the world of books and exposure to 'book' language.

You can read about many more activities and resources for babies in *A Practical Guide to Activities for Young Children,* including 'treasure baskets'. (A treasure basket is a container filled with objects made of natural materials. It can be given to a baby to stimulate all the senses.)

Good practice in working with babies

1 Listening and responding to very young children is a priority. Some time should be spent with each one every day on a one-to-one basis.
2 Books should be available at all times and care should be taken to choose those most suitable for the age group.
3 All children, however young, need stimulating play.
4 Children in nappies should be changed as soon as the nappies become wet or soiled.
5 Babies should be allowed to sleep at the time they wish and not have to fit in with the daily routine.
6 Toilet-training should take place only after discussion with the parents and when the child shows she is ready to be trained, not just to fit in with the daily routine.
7 The 'key worker' system should be part of the practice of the placement.
8 Clear records and observations need to be kept and shared with the family.

Toddlers

Toddlers should be given every opportunity to explore and set their own agenda within a safe environment. Some toddlers may be walking confidently by their first birthday, while others may need encouragement to get started. There are many toys that can be provided to help with walking, such as baby walkers, trucks and trolleys which can by pushed along. Balls of all sizes, made out of various materials, stimulate a toddler to move and also extend the mobility of children who are already walking by aiding their balance and co-ordination. As toddlers become more proficient at walking, so pull-along toys become more fun, and encourage them to walk for longer periods.

Equipment for children between one and two years old can include a small slide which allows them to practise climbing the steps – sliding down is the reward! 'Hidey hole' boxes or large wooden cubes, which are sturdy and large enough for toddlers to climb into, promote skills of getting in and out of objects, co-ordination and balance. Strong supermarket cartons are an acceptable alternative.

Wheeled toys that toddlers can sit on and move with their feet, encourage them to practise steering skills, balance, co-ordination and to help them strengthen leg muscles. A low climbing frame aids balance and co-ordination and strengthens arm and leg muscles, as do balls for throwing, catching and kicking. Outings to parks, where the playground may have swings, seesaws, roundabouts and rocking toys, are enjoyable. Here, children can use the equipment according to their own individual skills, under close supervision.

There are many materials that will help develop manipulative skills and hand–eye co-ordination such as: bricks for building towers that can be knocked down; stacking cups and beakers; small tins and cartons that can be improvised from around the house; posting boxes; hammer sets; dolls that are easily undressed; and simple inset jigsaws.

During the second year, as the child becomes mobile and understands more, she has to learn how to fit happily into the family and the larger outside environment and a set of rules has to be learnt about acceptable behaviour. Although play at this stage is solitary, the presence of a familiar adult provides reassurance and security. A toddler is not interested in playing co-operatively with other children. She has just learnt the meaning of 'mine', and the concept of sharing usually does not occur until the third year.

Learning accelerates as the toddler becomes more proficient with language. Although play is mainly solitary, she spends an increasingly large proportion of her time in exploratory and experimental play; in looking at books; listening to, and taking part in songs and rhymes; learning that objects have names, as do parts of the body; and realising that by using language, needs are met without having recourse to pointing and whingeing. Opportunities should be found for conversation and good communication, taking time to listen as well as talk. Providing interest tables, displaying pictures and posters, allowing toddlers to handle objects; all these things will stimulate their curiosity, as well as helping to extend their vocabulary. You can read much more about providing activities and resources for toddlers in *A Practical Guide to Activities for Young Children*.

Toddlers always need to be closely supervised. Their natural curiosity and adventurousness will lead them to potentially dangerous activities, so their environment needs to be as hazard-free as possible. All toys and equipment need to be durable and bought from a reputable manufacturer, and need to be checked for damage, maintained and repaired if necessary. Make sure that anything they are playing with cannot be swallowed or inserted into ears or up noses. Then you will not need to restrict their natural instinct to explore with their senses – this includes touching and taking items to their mouths.

Good practice in working with toddlers

1 A hazard-free environment is of the utmost importance at this age, as toddlers need freedom to explore safely.
2 Toddlers need routines as this helps them to feel secure. These should be flexible as rigid rules might cause anxiety.
3 Toddlers need time to act for themselves. Independence is encouraged when the time is taken to allow them to dress and feed themselves.

4 Toddlers thrive in an affectionate atmosphere, where adults show interest in them, respond appropriately to their attempts at speech, and understand their body language.
5 Toddlers need boundaries and calm consistent care that allows them to express themselves safely. Challenging behaviour is met with the same response from all the carers in the establishment.
6 Toddlers can become very attached to the adults in the nursery. Students need to be aware of this, and discuss their approach with their supervisor.

The role of the student

Children learn from everything they do. Everything you see in your placement will contribute to their learning, whether it is:

- preparing and sitting down to eat a leisurely meal with the children
- involving them in domestic tasks, such as clearing up, shopping and gardening
- going for a walk in the park
- all the play activities you plan, indoors and out
- describing and talking about any of the routines you carry out with the children.

All activities and experiences the children are involved in should be suitable for their stage of development. You should think about:

- the child's current stage of development
- what the child can already do
- what she has achieved so far
- the child's interests and preferences.

Children develop at different rates and it is not helpful to compare children with one another. Learning outcomes should not be seen as the only goals for children. Many children are capable of much more and of much wider learning.

All research has shown that close partnership between educators, carers and parents encourages children's learning and development.

CASE STUDY

Mel is in an Infant School, working with six year olds. Three times a week the class visits the IT room, where several computers have been set up. Mel has been asked to help any child who finds it difficult to use a computer. She dreads these sessions, as she has not admitted to her supervisor that she has never been able to come to terms with computers and that the children are all much better than she is.

1 What steps can Mel take to feel more competent?
2 Should she discuss her problem with her supervisor?
3 Who else might she talk to?

Students involved in children's play and practical activities have an important and sensitive role to play. You need to be aware of the value of all activities to the children's development and learning, and plan and prepare them thoroughly. There should be enough material provided for the entire group to take part in the activity. You should never make models, paint or draw pictures for children, as this will stunt their imagination – they will suppose that as an adult you can do better than they, and will then only copy what you have done. Remember, it is the process of creative work that is most important in children's learning, not what they produce at the end.

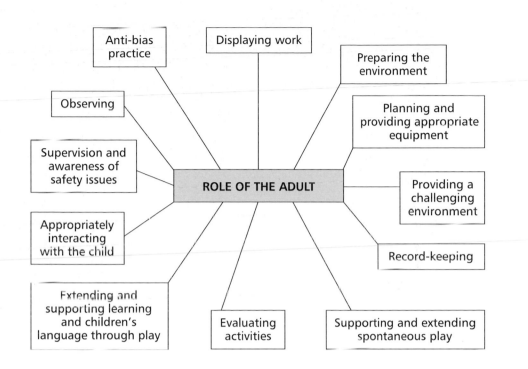

There has to be enough space for the children. They should have the chance to do the activity if they want to. Young children should never be forced into doing an activity if they do not wish to. On the other hand, a child who refuses at first, might well want to join in later on.

There is also the question of enough time. It is obviously not sensible to start a creative art activity that will take about an hour or more, just before the dinner break. You will also have to fit in with the time that your supervisor has given you.

All activities need to be supervised for safety reasons. Even playing with water can lead to a slippery floor and an unnecessary accident. Other activities, such as woodwork, cooking and outside play, have obvious built-in hazards, so need to be carefully planned and closely supervised. If there are small babies or toddlers in your placement, even more care must be taken. Small beads, Lego® bricks or broken items, for example, need to be put out of the way in order to avoid choking accidents. Scissors, needles and knives should never be used or left lying around near babies.

All the activities you plan need to be suitable and accessible to all the children in your care. All the resources you use need to be checked so that they promote positive images of all cultures, disability and both genders. Sometimes you will find boys dominating the outdoor play, whilst the girls take over the Home Corner. This is not acceptable, and the placement should make sure that all children take part in all activities. If there are children with disabilities in your placement, they must be included in all activities.

Whatever the activity, you will be there as a resource, to provide materials, time and space, and to take part when necessary. For example, in imaginary play, you should only take part if invited, whereas in cooking your presence is essential, in providing support, instruction and supervision.

Whenever you provide an activity, having planned, prepared and carried it out, you will need to think about the learning and development of the children and how you might do it even better next time. Talk to your supervisor about what you have done – and be prepared to accept constructive criticism. Even if something goes disastrously wrong, you will have learnt from it, and it is not the end of the world!

1 Who was mainly at fault?
2 How can Monica put the matter right?
3 What should she do next time she is asked to supervise an activity?
4 How should the supervisor have reacted?

All activities should encourage the children's all-round development. Through your knowledge of the children and how they develop, you will be able to plan activities with the children's needs in mind. This will help you to be aware of what is happening and when you need to step in to move the play forward. There will be many occasions when unstructured and spontaneous activities will be fun for all concerned, and allow children to use their imagination. There are very few activities that do not have some value. You should always be aware of the value of the activities you are planning and preparing.

GOOD PRACTICE IN HELPING CHILDREN TO LEARN

1 Talk with children frequently, listen to them carefully and discuss their questions fully.
2 Encourage them to concentrate on activities so as to extend their concentration span.
3 Encourage them to share and join in activities with other children, so as to promote co-operation in the class.
4 Tell them stories, and read and talk about books with them whenever possible.
5 Encourage them to look at books by themselves.
6 Share songs and number rhymes; and look for an opportunity to teach them new songs.
7 Provide plenty of well-sharpened pencils and crayons, and give them time and opportunity to incorporate writing into their play.
8 Introduce and explain as much new vocabulary as possible.
9 Encourage counting and the use of numbers in all situations.
10 Spell words correctly and write clearly.
11 Praise children for their efforts and show them that you appreciate all their achievements.

8 HEALTH AND SAFETY

> **This chapter covers:**
> ■ **Safety in the placement**
> ■ **Personal health and hygiene**
> ■ **Children with HIV**

Under the Health and Safety at Work Act of 1974, employers have a duty to provide healthy and safe working conditions. This chapter does not attempt to describe the total responsibilities of any placement in providing such an environment. It is intended simply as a guide to assist you in your role of contributing to a healthy and safe environment.

Safety in the placement

When you start working in any placement you need to discover the following information as soon as possible. Written policies held by the placement should help you in this task.

CHECKLIST – FIRE

■ What is the procedure to follow should a fire occur?
■ Where are the fire alarms?
■ What type of alarm is used?
■ How are the children taken from the building?
■ What exits are used? Under what circumstances?
■ Where do you gather outside the building?
■ Where are the registers kept? (The children's names need to be checked when everyone is out of the building.)

You should find that there are regular fire drills, in each placement, to make sure everyone knows what to do in the event of a fire.

CHECKLIST – ACCIDENTS

■ What is the procedure to follow should an accident occur?

- What is the policy for recording both minor and major accidents?
- Who is responsible for informing the parent/carer of any accident?
- Where is the first aid box kept?
- Who is responsible for checking the contents? How often is this done, and is the checking recorded?
- What does the first aid box contain?
- Do any of the dressings have an expiry date on them?
- Are there any lotions, creams or disinfectants in the box? If so, what are they?
- Who has a first aid qualification?
- Who are the named first-aiders?
- Who is the appointed person to take charge in the event of an accident?
- Where is the nearest telephone?

Children are the responsibility of the adults who care for them. An accident is something that happens that is not expected and may be prevented with care and thought. Sometimes accidents occur because the carer is in a hurry; is experiencing stress due to personal problems; or is feeling tired and therefore less alert.

Every accident, however slight, should be reported and recorded in the accident book. Ask your supervisor if you can look at the book. You will see that very full details are recorded. This information is necessary, as some seemingly minor accidents can result in more serious concerns so an

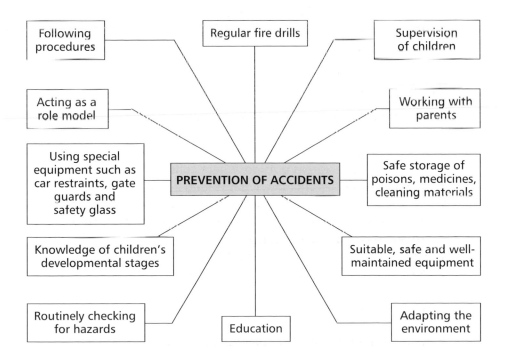

accurate record can be vital. The accident book may also show hazards that occur regularly. Remember, too, that parents must be informed of any injury, however slight it may seem.

CHECKLIST – OTHER ESSENTIAL INFORMATION

- What is the procedure concerning storage and administration of medicine? (Not all placements are prepared to accept this responsibility.)
- Do any of the doors exit on to a main road? Is there a procedure for making sure children do not have access to this?
- Find out the procedure for dealing with an outbreak of infection.
- Find out how the outside play area is set up. Find out how risks from falls and collisions are minimized indoors and out.

THE ENVIRONMENT

All children are entitled to a clean, safe, pleasant, caring environment. As a student, you can contribute to this by being alert to hazards and giving thought to your practice. If you have identified a problem or hazard, discuss it with your supervisor as soon as possible.

CHECKLIST – HAZARDS

- Are any toys or items of equipment damaged or faulty?
- Is all the furniture safe and secure?
- Are there any electrical points uncovered, any trailing wires or unofficial wiring?
- Are cleaning substances and medicines kept locked away, out of the reach of children?
- Are there hidden areas outside, where children cannot be seen?
- Are electric kettles and mugs of hot fluid kept out of the reach of children?
- Are there any poisonous plants inside or outside the placement?
- Are all pets in a healthy condition?
- Are there any obstructions in corridors and doorways?
- Are fire doors left closed, as they should be?
- Is there any rubbish or paper lying around, increasing the risk of fire?
- Is the outdoor play equipment safe and checked regularly?

All safety equipment should meet British standards and carry the appropriate British Standard mark. All new equipment should meet the British Standard/European CE safety standard. Manufacturers' instructions and guidelines for any piece of safety equipment should be kept where they can be referred to easily. All equipment must be used according to the guidelines.

Passive smoking

Passive smoking is a serious health risk to babies, children, and adults. Because of this, smoking has not been permitted in registered settings for some time. In July 2007, new legislation made it illegal to smoke in enclosed public places and workplaces in England, prompting many smokers to give up. Not only does this ensure a healthier environment for us all, it also means that children are less likely to see adult role models smoking.

GOOD PRACTICE IN MAINTAINING A SAFE ENVIRONMENT

1 The room should be aired regularly and a temperature of 20°C maintained.
2 The eating area should be clean, attractive and free from any debris. Clean up well after meals.
3 Following placement procedure, change any child who is soiled or wet at once, maintaining personal hygiene.
4 Following placement procedure, use the correct procedure for disposing of nappies and soiled clothing.

Safety labels

Label	Name	Meaning	Where found – Placement

5 Do not allow small areas of the room to become overcrowded or cluttered. Organize activities so that noise levels are controlled.
6 Maintain a clean, soft area where children can rest on pillows or rugs.
7 Shut gates and doors properly behind you.
8 Use stair gates where appropriate.
9 Wipe spills of water or food at once, and do not allow the children to walk on floors recently washed in case they slip.
10 Keep pets in a healthy condition, regularly cleaning cages and hutches.
11 Prevent children in outside play areas from talking to strangers who may attempt to attract their attention.
12 Regularly wash dressing-up clothes and cushion covers, toys and equipment.
13 Make sure that children work and play in well-lit areas.
14 Wear sensible shoes with flat heels for work.
15 Some activities in the placement are potentially dangerous. Children working with wood or cooking should be closely supervised at all times. Discuss your proposed activities thoroughly with your supervisor beforehand, so that you are alerted to all the risks.

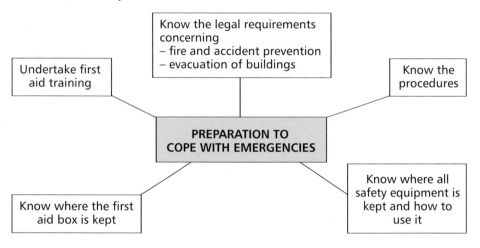

Undertake first aid training

Know the legal requirements concerning
– fire and accident prevention
– evacuation of buildings

Know the procedures

PREPARATION TO COPE WITH EMERGENCIES

Know where the first aid box is kept

Know where all safety equipment is kept and how to use it

Activity
With the permission of your supervisor, look at the placement accident book.
1 How many accidents have occurred in the last six months?
2 List the different types of accident.
3 Is there a pattern to the accidents?
4 What first aid procedures were used?

Whilst you are on your course, you are likely to be attending a first aid course, which will allow you to deal with all emergencies in a professional manner.

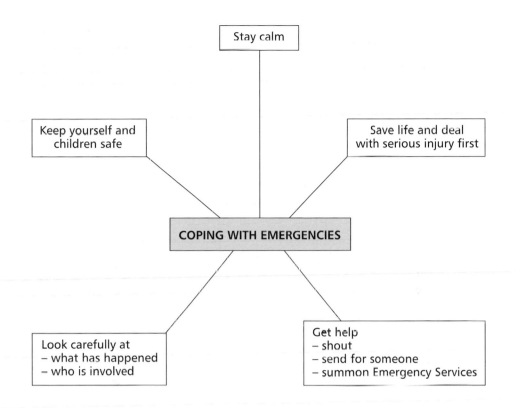

Personal health and hygiene

There are many definitions of health. The World Health Organization (WHO) states that 'Health is a state of complete physical, mental and social well-being, not merely the absence of disease or infirmity.' It involves children, families and the community, and is a positive goal, not just the absence of illness.

You should present yourself as a good role model and encourage the children to think about their health in a positive way. On your course, you will look at the concept of health and health education. This knowledge should be demonstrated and displayed in your practice at all times.

Infection is the most common cause of illness in young children and, if frequent, can cause developmental delay and prevent growth. Infection can range from the common cold to more serious infections such as meningitis. As students, it is important to know not only how infection is spread but also your role in preventing its spread.

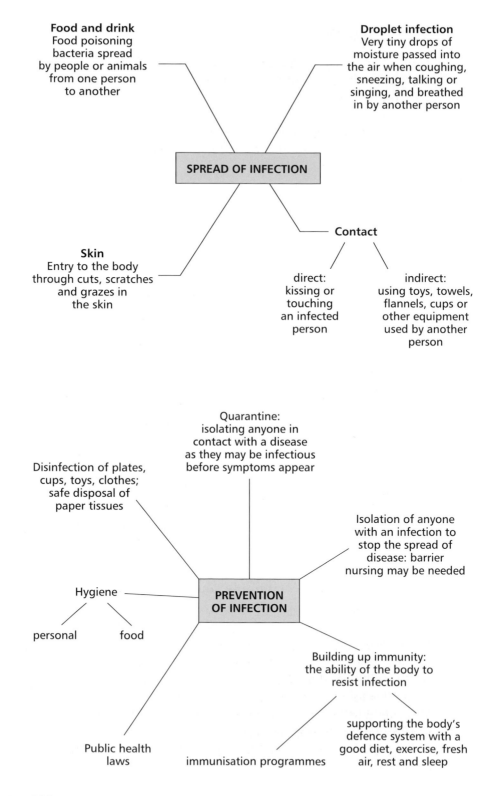

Food and drink
Food poisoning
bacteria spread
by people or animals
from one person
to another

Droplet infection
Very tiny drops of
moisture passed into
the air when coughing,
sneezing, talking or
singing, and breathed
in by another person

SPREAD OF INFECTION

Skin
Entry to the body
through cuts, scratches
and grazes in
the skin

Contact

direct:
kissing or
touching
an infected
person

indirect:
using toys, towels,
flannels, cups or
other equipment
used by another
person

Quarantine:
isolating anyone in
contact with a disease
as they may be infectious
before symptoms appear

Disinfection of plates,
cups, toys, clothes;
safe disposal of
paper tissues

Isolation of anyone
with an infection to
stop the spread of
disease: barrier
nursing may be needed

Hygiene

**PREVENTION
OF INFECTION**

personal   food

Building up immunity:
the ability of the body to
resist infection

Public health
laws

immunisation programmes

supporting the body's
defence system with a
good diet, exercise, fresh
air, rest and sleep

Susie is in placement in a private day nursery. Tom, aged two, starts to cry and is picked up for a cuddle. Suddenly he vomits all over Susie's clothes and shoes, and screams hysterically.

1 What is the first thing that Susie should do?
2 What is the best way of dealing with the mess?
3 How can Tom be comforted?
4 Should the parents be informed immediately?
5 What help will Susie need?

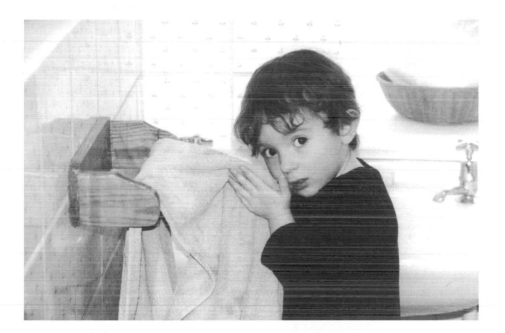

GOOD PRACTICE IN PERSONAL HYGIENE

1 Encourage all children to wash their hands after using the lavatory, and before eating or taking part in cooking activities. Washing hands thoroughly means rolling up your sleeves, using warm rather than cold water, applying soap to wet hands, both backs and fronts, between the fingers and around the fingertips, rinsing well and drying preferably with a disposable towel. Both you and the children should follow this procedure.
2 Play your part in making sure the lavatories are always clean and that soap and paper towels are available.
3 Dispose of rubbish such as dirty nappies or tissues promptly and correctly.

4 Be careful not to lift anything that is too heavy for you or to allow the children to do so.
5 Do not allow smoking in the same room as the children.
6 If you are responsible for food preparation, remember the importance of clean working surfaces and utensils, strict personal hygiene and food storage. Do not handle food if you have an infected cut or diarrhoea.
7 Encourage children to cover their mouths if they cough.
8 Teach children to blow their noses with a tissue, then dispose of the tissue correctly.
9 You may well come into contact with children who have rubella (German measles). If you are a young woman, planning to have a family later in life, check if you are immune to rubella before starting the course. If you have no rubella antibodies, become pregnant and then contract rubella, there is a risk of your baby being damaged.
10 Keep up with new research and developments, for example the risk of covering fatty food with cling film.

CASE STUDY

Karen is enjoying her nursery placement and building good caring relationships with the children. She picks them up when they cry and cuddles them when they ask her for close contact.

In the second week of her placement, she is horrified to find that she has nits. She tells her supervisor who informs her that there are three children in the nursery who are infested with head lice. The parents have been informed.

1 Should Karen have been told?
2 Do you think that an infestation of nits is a rare or a common event in a nursery?
3 What steps should Karen take now to get rid of them?
4 How can she protect herself in future?

Children with HIV (Human Immunodeficiency Virus)

Blood-borne viruses can only be transmitted through an exchange of body fluids. HIV, hepatitis B and hepatitis C are examples of blood-bourne viruses.

It is possible that, in your placement, there may be a child who is HIV positive; a situation of which you may or may not be aware. Many children who are HIV positive remain well and healthy, displaying no symptoms of AIDS (Acquired Immune Deficiency Syndrome). Children with an impaired immune system may have a greater risk of catching infections and may also experience severe complications from common childhood infections, such as measles and chickenpox.

The virus is extremely fragile and unable to survive long outside the body. It cannot be carried through the air. It is destroyed by heat, light, bleach and detergents. The main routes of transmission are through sexual contact, blood-to-blood through sharing needles and syringes, and from mother to baby. There is no known case of HIV being transmitted in any child-care setting. Most pathogens, such as hepatitis B, are much more infectious than the HIV virus.

Good hygiene practice plays an important part in providing a safe and caring environment for children. All children should be treated as if they were HIV positive, and this will ensure good practice and equal treatment for all. If good hygiene practices are followed, you will not need to be overly anxious. Settings will have written procedures covering the prevention of cross-infection through body fluids (blood, urine, faeces and saliva).

In addition to the good hygiene practices previously discussed, you should:

- wash blood, faeces and urine off your skin with hot water and soap
- regularly clean and disinfect floors, equipment, toys and cups
- clean up any spilt blood or faeces with a bleach solution (one part household bleach to ten parts water, known as a 'one to ten bleach solution')
- cover any open wounds on your skin or on a child's skin
- wear disposable gloves when dealing with faeces, urine or blood
- rinse well with running water for several minutes if blood is splashed on your face or in your eyes
- soak any blooded clothes, or implements used for first aid, in a one to ten bleach solution for 5–10 minutes
- wipe the nappy changing pad with a one to ten bleach solution after each use
- double wrap all waste that contains body fluids, then put it in plastic sacks.

It is recommended that all practitioners become immunised against hepatitis B. This entails three injections given in the arm. There is currently no immunisation for hepatitis C or HIV.

Children can only grow and develop if they are protected. As you develop your skills and knowledge, you will understand that good child-care practice includes the prevention of accidents and illness, and being prepared to deal with emergencies in a calm, organized and confident manner.

9 PROVIDING FOOD AND DRINK

> **This chapter covers:**
> - **A healthy diet**
> - **Feeding babies**
> - **Special diets**
> - **Emotional and cultural influences**
> - **Food hygiene**
> - **Mealtimes**

Eating patterns are established at a very early age. Part of your role in caring for children will include providing food and drink, educating them in eating healthily, understanding the main rules of nutrition, and being a good role model by setting a good example when you are eating with the children.

A healthy diet

A healthy diet consists of a variety of foods. Care must be taken to eat sufficient to meet your needs but not to overeat, particularly saturated fats and sugars. The more energetic you are, the more calories (units of energy) you will burn up, and the more food you will need. Energy is required by all living things to maintain the changes and chemical reactions that occur in the body (metabolism).

Foods that have little water and a high proportion of fat or carbohydrate have a high energy value. Children need more kilocalories because their bodies are growing and they use a lot of energy. The kilocalories required will vary according to age, gender, size, physical activity and climate.

The chart opposite from *A Practical Guide to Child Nutrition*, by Angela Dare and Margaret O'Donovan, clearly shows how a balanced diet promotes health and development.

A variety of fresh foods daily in adequate amounts, from the following food groups, should be offered to children every day:
- Bread, cereal, rice and pasta.
- Vegetables and fruits.

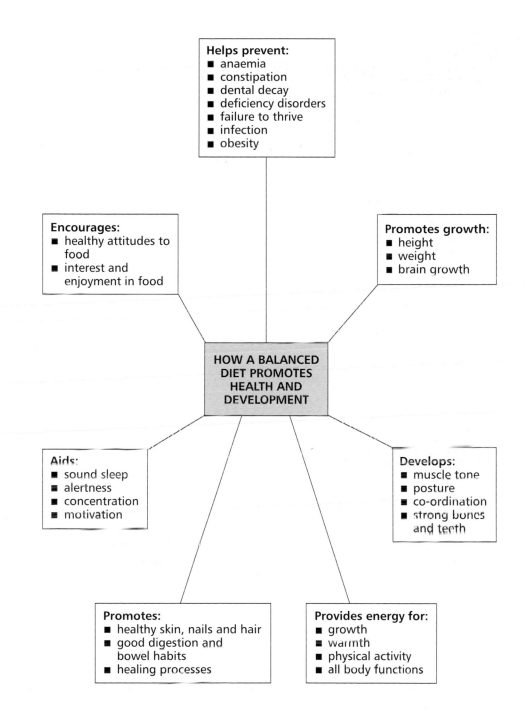

Helps prevent:
- anaemia
- constipation
- dental decay
- deficiency disorders
- failure to thrive
- infection
- obesity

Encourages:
- healthy attitudes to food
- interest and enjoyment in food

Promotes growth:
- height
- weight
- brain growth

HOW A BALANCED DIET PROMOTES HEALTH AND DEVELOPMENT

Aids:
- sound sleep
- alertness
- concentration
- motivation

Develops:
- muscle tone
- posture
- co-ordination
- strong bones and teeth

Promotes:
- healthy skin, nails and hair
- good digestion and bowel habits
- healing processes

Provides energy for:
- growth
- warmth
- physical activity
- all body functions

- Fats and sugars.
- Milk, yoghurt and cheese.
- Meat, poultry, fish, eggs, beans and pulses.

Children have different food needs to adults to allow for their healthy growth and development. No single food can supply all the nutrients required by a child.

There is a view that some children, particularly the younger ones, or children that are unwell, benefit if they eat little and often. Snacks should certainly be offered if children are hungry but try to discourage children from snacking less than two hours before a meal as it might spoil their appetite for the main meal. Some examples of wholesome and enjoyable snacks are:

- water, milk and fresh fruit juices (diluted with water to prevent tooth enamel rotting)
- fresh fruit
- dried fruit such as apricots (a good source of iron), prunes and figs
- vegetable sticks, such as carrots, celery and cucumber
- hummus
- yoghurt
- crackers
- oatmeal biscuits
- rice cakes.

Use sugar in moderation, as sugar can lead to tooth decay and excess weight (obesity). If you are cooking with the children, try to cook something other than cakes and biscuits. Salt should be used sparingly in cooking, and should not be put on the table for children to help themselves.

Feeding babies

Babies' first food is milk. This can be breast milk or formula (dried cow's milk, enriched with vitamins, and given in a bottle).

BOTTLE FEEDS

Formula milk is usually made from cow's milk, where the protein and fat levels have been altered and vitamins and minerals added. Like a breast-fed baby, the baby should be allowed to dictate its feeding requirements to allow for changes in appetite and growth.

Studies have shown that bottle-fed babies are frequently given feeds that are over or under concentrated. If you are asked to prepare a bottle for a baby, always read and follow the instructions, as manufacturers often develop and change their products.

1 Check that the formula has not passed its sell by date. Read the instructions on the tin. Ensure the tin has been kept in a cool, dry cupboard.

2 Boil some **fresh** water and allow to cool.

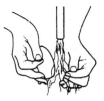

3 Wash hands and nails thoroughly.

4 Take required equipment from sterilizing tank and rinse with cool, boiled water.

5 Fill bottle, or a jug if making a large quantity, to the required level with water.

6 Measure the exact amount of powder using the scoop provided. Level with a knife. **Do not pack down**.

7 Add the powder to the measured water in the bottle or jug.

8 Screw cap on bottle and shake, or mix well in the jug and pour into sterilized bottles.

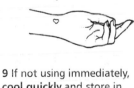

9 If not using immediately, **cool quickly** and store in the fridge. If using immediately, test temperature on the inside of your wrist.

10 Babies will take cold milk but they prefer warm food (as from the breast). If you wish to warm the milk, place bottle in a jug of hot water. **Never keep warm for longer than 45 minutes** to reduce chances of bacteria breeding.

Note Whenever the bottle is left for short periods, or stored in the fridge, cover with the cap provided.

Preparing the bottle feed

All equipment (bottles, teats, bottle tops, scoops) used for bottle-feeding should be sterile as germs thrive on milk. Sterilization of this equipment usually involves using a chemical agent such as Milton®, a particular disinfectant for keeping bottles free from bacteria. Bottles and equipment may also be boiled, in which case they need to be kept under the boiling water for at least ten minutes. You should always make sure you have washed your hands thoroughly before preparing bottles.

1 Wash the bottles, teats and other equipment in hot water and detergent. Use a bottle brush for the inside of bottles. **Do not rub salt on the teats**. Squeeze boiled water through the teats.

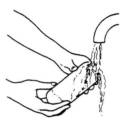

2 Rinse everything thoroughly in clean running water.

3 Fill the sterilizer with clean, cold water. Add chemical solution. If in a tablet form, allow to dissolve.

4 Put the bottles, teats and other equipment (nothing metal) into the water. Ensure everything is covered completely by the water, with no bubbles. If necessary, weight down. Leave for the required time according to manufacturer's instructions.

Sterilization of bottles using a chemical solution

When giving a feed, both you and the baby need to be comfortable and look at each other, and you should speak softly and encouragingly to the baby. Never leave the baby on her own with a bottle (prop feeding), as this is very dangerous as she might choke.

WEANING

In a family placement or nursery you may see babies being introduced to solid food (weaning). This is generally between the ages of four to six months, by which time the baby's digestive system is more able to cope with a variety of food. The milk diet alone might not be satisfying a baby, and she might be waking hungry during the night.

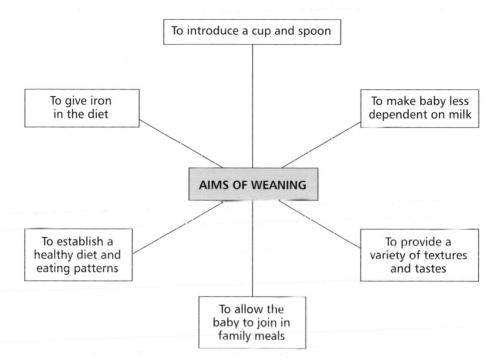

| To introduce a cup and spoon |
| To give iron in the diet |
| To make baby less dependent on milk |

AIMS OF WEANING

| To establish a healthy diet and eating patterns |
| To provide a variety of textures and tastes |
| To allow the baby to join in family meals |

From six months solid food becomes important for growth and the prevention of anaemia. From this age foods that can be held by the baby (finger foods) and food that is no longer puréed but just mashed may be introduced. Finger foods could include pieces of carrot and apple, crusts of bread or rice biscuits. Babies should have their own plate and spoon. This equipment does not have to be sterilized, but should be kept very clean.

CASE STUDY

It was snack time in a small private nursery. While the children were given juice to drink, the student, Sylvia, handed a plate of biscuits round. Theo, aged six months, thoroughly enjoyed his biscuit – a new experience for him. Sylvia told Theo's mother how much the baby had enjoyed his snack time. On hearing that Theo had eaten a biscuit, his mother was furious as she did not want her baby to have anything to eat in the nursery that she had not provided herself, and thought she had made this clear to the staff.

1 Why do you think the mother was angry that her baby was given a biscuit?
2 How might this situation have been prevented?
3 Who was at fault?
4 What should Sylvia check next time she is handing out snacks?

All mealtimes, especially those for a baby, should take place in a quiet, calm atmosphere. New tastes should be encouraged without ever forcing them upon her. If the baby dislikes something on a Monday, she may well enjoy it the following Friday. It is always worthwhile re-introducing foods, as the baby's tastes become more mature. Babies should be encouraged to enjoy their food, allowed to help by holding a spoon, given 'finger foods', and no fuss should be made if there is any mess.

Special diets

Some children that you care for may be on a special diet, particularly if you are placed in a special school. Special diets are worked out by the doctor and dietician according to the individual needs of the child (see table opposite). Nurseries and schools have to work closely with parents in order to provide the correct diet for the child. You will be told during your placement if a child is on a special diet. It is important that you find out as much as you can about the condition, and encourage and support the child.

Common disorders that require a special diet

Condition	Description	Diet
Coeliac disease	Sensitivity to gluten, a protein found in wheat, rye, barley and oats. Child fails to thrive	Excluding all foods containing gluten. Can eat fresh fruit and vegetables, fish, meat and dairy produce
Cystic fibrosis	An inherited condition, sticky thick mucus is found in the lungs and digestive system. Interferes with the digestion of food	Tablets given to help the digestion. Needs a high protein, high calorie diet
Diabetes	The body fails to produce enough insulin to control the amount of sugar in the body	Regular meals, diet carefully balanced and controlled. May need a snack before exercise, should be observed closely
Obesity	Overweight for height and age	Plan, offer and encourage a healthy balanced diet. Discourage over-eating. Encourage daily exercise
Anaemia	Lack of iron in the diet. Can also be caused by severe blood loss	A diet high in red meat, liver, eggs, cocoa, green vegetables, apricots, helped by taking Vitamin C at the same time
Cow's milk allergy: • to protein	Association with family history of allergy. Can result in wheezing, diarrhoea, vomiting, rashes,	Special formula milk for babies. Substitute milks for older children.

Under no circumstances must you give the child anything that she is not allowed. You will need to tell your supervisor if the whole meal provided is not eaten.

Emotional and cultural influences

There are several influences on the way we eat, and our preferences are determined by the way we feel, the food provided in the family and the culture around us.

EMOTIONAL FACTORS

The amount we eat is often influenced by our emotions, some of us eating more and some of us less. If we are unhappy, we often 'comfort eat', devouring large amounts of sweet or starchy food. When in love, we are often unable to eat at all.

For the majority of us, offering food is a way of expressing love. Toddlers soon learn the power they have if they refuse to eat. It is a sure-fire way to wind up her parent or carer! No child has ever starved to death by refusing one or two meals, and the sensible person will learn to ignore occasional food refusal and just remove the plate in a calm manner.

When a child is not feeling happy and secure, she might find it difficult to eat and may lose her appetite for a while. Again, a little patience and a

willingness to listen to the child's problems usually helps to restore the child's appetite. On the other hand, an unhappy child might overeat, thus risking obesity, and perhaps becoming more isolated. Take care when offering food as a comfort.

Some adults have emotional reactions to the look of certain types of food, so it is not surprising if children do as well. Presenting all food in an attractive way may encourage children to eat foods they normally refuse. Offering small amounts rather than full plates may also help children to regain their appetites.

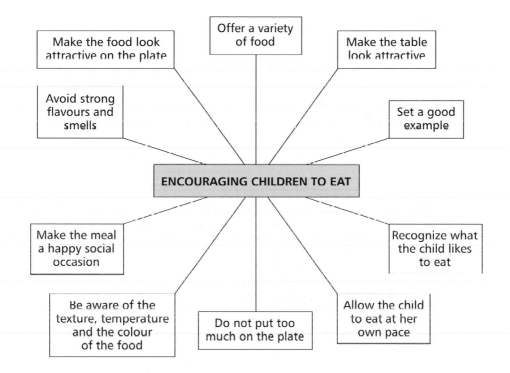

CULTURAL FACTORS

Most schools and nurseries provide food from many cultures. This benefits the children by:
- introducing them to new tastes
- helping them to develop an interest in and respect for other cultures
- providing a link between home and nursery/school for some children.

Many diets are linked to religious practices. The table on page 120 indicates the main religions and the foods they do not eat.

Dietary customs

Food	Jewish	Sikh	Muslim	Hindu	Buddhist	7th Day Adventist	Rastafarian	Roman Catholic	Mormon
eggs	no blood spots	×	×	some	some	most	×	×	×
milk/yoghurt	not with meat	×	not with rennet	not with rennet	×	most	×		×
cheese	not with meat	some	some	some	×	most	×	×	×
chicken	kosher	some	halal	some	±	some	some	some still prefer not to eat meat on Fridays particularly during Lent	×
mutton/lamb	kosher	×	halal	some	±	some	some		×
beef	kosher	±	halal	±	±	some	some		×
pork	±	rarely	× ±	rarely	±	±	±		×
fish	with scales, fins and back-bone	some	halal ±	with fins and scales	some	some	×	×	×
shellfish	±	some	halal	some	±	±	±	×	×
animal fats	kosher	some	some halal	some	±	±	some	×	×
alcohol	×	×	±	±	±	±	±	×	±
cocoa/tea/coffee	×	×	×	×	× no milk	±	×	×	±
nuts	×	×	×	×	×	×	×	×	×
pulses	×	×	×	×	×	×	×	×	×
fruit	×	×	×	×	×	×	×	×	×
vegetables	×	×	×	×	×	×	×	×	×
fasting (where not specified, fasting is a matter of individual choice)	Yom Kippur		Ramadan						24 hours once monthly

You should never assume that because one of the children is from a certain ethnic group that she will necessarily eat certain foods or reject others. The placement will follow the guidelines given by the parents.

Some religions have special days when food is forbidden. This must always be respected and allowance made for the children feeling tired. They may need to rest more during the day and avoid strenuous physical activity.

Food hygiene

Many foods carry bacteria that grow in warm, moist conditions.

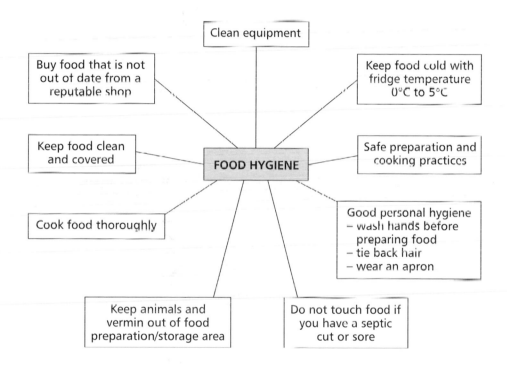

When caring for children it is important that you have very high standards of personal hygiene and an awareness of how to store and prepare food correctly in order to prevent infection. You must be sure that you and the children wash your hands after using the lavatory, handling animals and their equipment, coughing or sneezing, and before preparing and eating food. In addition, you need to wash your hands thoroughly after changing nappies, wiping noses, wiping bottoms and handling raw food. Never touch food if you have been suffering from vomiting or diarrhoea.

Symptoms of food poisoning can include diarrhoea, vomiting and stomach ache. Babies must be seen by a doctor immediately; and older children after 24 hours if they have not recovered. Children must be encouraged to drink water to replace water loss.

Mealtimes

Eating is a basic human need and an activity that most people enjoy. Apart from being essential for survival, it makes you feel good. Eating round the table is a social activity, a time when relaxed conversations can take place, and news shared.

Your placement will probably provide a range of eating utensils for the children, and they should then become skilled at using chopsticks as well as knives and forks. 'Table manners' are more important in some schools and nurseries than in others. Appetites differ in children and are unpredictable. Children know their own hunger signs and it is more sensible to offer smaller portions, providing more later if the child requests it.

Children have a shorter attention span than adults. Some find it very hard to sit at the table. It might be a good idea to allow these children to leave the table when they have finished, providing a quiet activity for them so as not to disturb others who are slower. Let children eat at their own pace.

Some children cause anxiety because they may:

- refuse to eat many foods
- take a long time to eat their food
- refuse to swallow food
- display other poor eating behaviours.

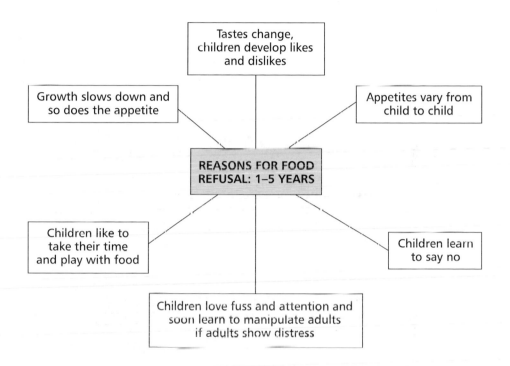

If a child is causing anxiety, make a record of what food is being refused, how she behaves at the table (such as crying, complaining or throwing food) and what food she enjoys. You may see a pattern, such as too many snacks prior to the meal, and so be able to resolve the problem. If the behaviour persists after you feel the child has settled into the nursery, and there is no obvious reason, your supervisor will need to involve the parents and discuss how she eats at home.

CASE STUDY

Ben, aged two-and-a-half years, has recently started to attend a full-time day nursery. The staff have formed a good relationship with Ben's mother and the settling in period has gone well. There appears to be one concern: Ben sits at the table for long periods of time, chewing the same mouthful of food over and over again. He leaves the table with most of the food still on the plate; the rest, still in his mouth, is later found in various places around the room.

1 Explain why this is a worrying situation.
2 Should the parents be told?
3 Why do you think Ben treats food in this way?
4 How can you help Ben to enjoy his food more?

There is a fashion today for some parents to allow their children to 'graze'. This means eating continually, on demand, and usually walking around with the food. Most placements will not be happy with this, and it will have to be discussed with the parents.

GOOD PRACTICE IN ENCOURAGING HEALTHY EATING HABITS

1 Let children help themselves to food at the table.
2 Allow children to help prepare food sometimes.
3 Encourage children to set the table and clear it.
4 Talk to children during the meal about the foods.
5 Do not make a fuss about accidents at the table, also let children help mop up the spills.
6 Present food in an interesting way, mixing colours, flavours and textures.
7 Make the table look attractive, with a clean cloth and perhaps a small jug of flowers.
8 Encourage children to try new foods, presenting one new food at a time, when they are not tired or ill.
9 Set a good example by sitting at the table with the children and showing your enjoyment of the food.
10 Never force children to eat new foods.
11 Never make children finish what is on their plates or insist they sit at the table until they do so.
12 Let children eat at their own pace.
13 Ignore fussy behaviour and praise hearty appetites.

Food is one of the pleasures of life. Although there are trends in eating, it would appear that a balanced diet for adults and children and eating in moderation is the healthiest option.

UNDERSTANDING CHILDREN'S BEHAVIOUR

This chapter covers:
- Factors that influence behaviour
- Common types of challenging behaviour
- Growing independence
- Managing unwanted behaviour

Behaviour is the way in which a person conducts himself or herself in relation to other people. It is the response to an action. Some behaviour – such as rudeness and defiance – is seen as 'bad' or challenging, whilst other behaviour – such as politeness and obedience – is seen as 'good'.

Behaviour is learnt through the child watching the people closest to her and the way they react to her, both verbally and non-verbally. Rewards and punishments shape behaviour. The reward may just be praise and encouragement, the punishment a disapproving look but each will have an effect. Many of your placements will have a policy on how to deal with challenging behaviour, so you should take the opportunity to read it as soon as possible.

CASE STUDY

Kirsten, a first year child-care and education student, is assisting in playground duty during her Infant School placement. She sees Barbara, aged five, being attacked by two other five year olds. Henry, aged eight, Barbara's brother, sees what is going on and rushes to her rescue. He hits one of the children so hard that he makes the child's nose bleed.

1 How should Kirsten respond to the situation?
2 Do you think Henry behaved well?
3 What else might he have done?
4 What should Kirsten say to the children?
5 Should Kirsten discuss this with her supervisor?

Knowledge of the normal development of children will help you to understand what behaviour is acceptable at what age and stage of development. For example, a toddler is not expected to be completely toilet-trained; but regularly wetting and soiling pants would be worrying behaviour in a five year old.

The children you meet in your placements will come from various backgrounds, perhaps a variety of cultures, with parents who may well differ in the expectations they have of their children's behaviour. For example, some parents might explain in great detail to the child what it is she is doing wrong, whilst others might be more of the 'do as I say, not as I do' school. Some parents might have different expectations of boys and of girls, allowing boys to be more physical and active, and expecting girls to 'behave like ladies'.

CASE STUDY

Pippa's placement is in a small private nursery. She becomes fond of Clive, aged four, who is a delightful child, always happy and helpful. However, his habit of never saying 'please' and 'thank you' really upsets her. It is clear that he is not expected to say them at home.

1 What action should Pippa take?
2 Should the staff insist that Clive says 'please' and 'thank you'?
3 Should they discuss this with Clive's parents?

Factors that influence behaviour

Most of the factors that influence behaviour are family based. This is because behaviour is learnt first in the family, as the earliest experiences have the greatest influence. These factors include:

- where the child is in the family, that is, whether the oldest, youngest or in the middle
- siblings
- expectations of the parents
- child-rearing practices
- influence of the extended family, such as grandparents, aunts and uncles
- opportunities for play within the family home
- abuse and neglect
- gender stereotyping, where girls are expected to be quiet and polite and boys to be rude and noisy.

Other events that affect the whole family may also influence behaviour. These might include a death in the family, a new baby, unemployment, divorce or separation.

Other factors can include the:

- personality of the child
- school
- peer group/friends
- media, such as watching violent films that might encourage fighting
- presence of a disability
- experience of discrimination.

Common types of challenging behaviour

Some types of behaviour are so common that all children exhibit one or more of them sometimes. Attention-seeking behaviour is one of the most common forms of challenging behaviour. Children need to be reassured that they are loved and cared for and, if they are not given attention, may seek it by being aggressive, angry, rude, swearing, showing off, or expressing their need through other types of worrying behaviour.

TEMPER TANTRUMS

About half of all two year olds have tantrums regularly, usually when they are with their parents, and very seldom when they are playing on their own or attending school or pre-school. Tantrums happen because children feel

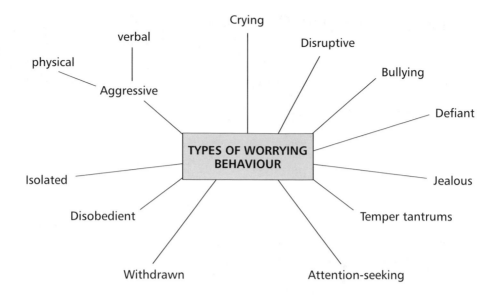

frustrated and need to get attention. Tantrums can be quite disturbing to watch. They need to be dealt with in the same way by both the carers and parents. If you see one coming, it is often possible to distract or divert the child. After the tantrum, the child may be frightened and need reassurance.

When the tantrum is over, cuddling the child and talking about feelings in a positive way should reduce the chance of further tantrums. It is harmful to slap, shake or handle a child roughly at any time but is even more so during a tantrum. Equally, giving in to the child and allowing her to manipulate you will increase the number of tantrums. Always report back to your supervisor and the child's parents if the child has had a severe tantrum.

JEALOUSY

It is an unusual family that never quarrels. Most children will fight from time to time. A new baby will sometimes arouse feelings of jealousy in an older child, who may show them in aggressive behaviour. Often, rivalry is expressed by quarrelling over toys and attention. In general, children can sort out most of these rows for themselves and unless they are doing serious damage to each other, it is often better to just let them get on with it.

While in your infant school placement, you may find a child who is jealous of the time her 'best friend' spends with other children. This needs careful handling but would make a good observation. Your supervisor would be interested to read about this and might have some helpful comments.

AGGRESSIVE BEHAVIOUR

Aggressive behaviour is one of the most difficult and challenging types of behaviour. It can be demonstrated in physical or verbal abuse towards staff, children or equipment. Younger children might scratch, pinch or bite and need to be made aware that this type of behaviour is not tolerated. You might need to spend some time explaining to children why this type of violent behaviour is unacceptable. It can be helpful to channel some aggression towards the dough or clay table.

Older children might bully younger or weaker children. This has to be tackled immediately. Your placement will have a written policy on how to deal with it. Always tell your supervisor if you see any instances of bullying.

WITHDRAWN BEHAVIOUR

Some children are naturally shy, quiet and rather reserved, unwilling to show affection or form close relationships. Up to a point, this should be respected but if the child is becoming isolated within the group, help might be needed. Sometimes withdrawal can be an indicator of abuse or neglect. Your careful observations of this behaviour could prove very useful.

PHYSICAL CAUSES

Sometimes problem behaviour has a physical cause. Lack of sleep can lead to a child being cross. Hunger can cause some children to lose concentration

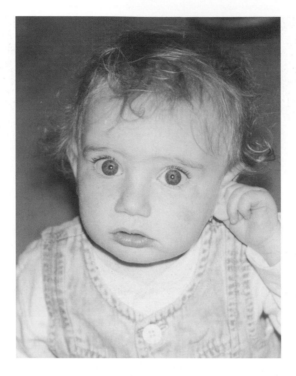

and become aggressive because their blood sugar level drops. Infection can cause changes in behaviour patterns. Having a hearing impairment might go undetected, and the placement staff might think the child lacks concentration.

COMFORT BEHAVIOUR

There are many forms of comfort behaviour, some more embarrassing than others. No one minds if a child drags a soft toy everywhere with her, whereas masturbating in public is not so acceptable. Sucking thumbs, dummies and pieces of material are all ways that children use to comfort themselves. They may become reliant on them at particular times of the day, usually at nap time and when confronted by a new or distressing situation. Not all children feel the need for a comfort object but, if a child has a comfort habit, you will have to tolerate it. It would be most upsetting for the child to have the object or the habit taken away suddenly. She will give it up in her own good time.

Other children might show their need for love and reassurance by displaying anxiety, fear or withdrawal, finding it difficult to express their feelings in the usual attention-seeking ways. Children need approval from adults, so as to believe that they are valued. If this is not forthcoming, their self-esteem will be low and they will find it difficult to learn and achieve.

Growing independence

There are some types of behaviour that are to be expected as part of the child's development.

CURIOSITY

As a baby becomes a toddler there will not be a cupboard that remains unexplored. Nor will there be a meal that is peaceful and does not have a messy end, with the toddler seeking to feed herself and enjoy the texture as well as the taste of food. Safety factors and constant supervision are of increasing importance, as the child's curiosity knows no limits.

BOREDOM

Children need stimulation and the opportunity to play and learn about the world around them. If they are restricted and frustrated, this will lead to boredom, perhaps resulting in attention-seeking behaviour.

Children these days are offered so many activities and play opportunities from a very young age that they sometimes find it hard to amuse themselves. It has been said that some 'boredom' is no bad thing, as it might help children to use their imagination or to concentrate on something that interests them.

Managing unwanted behaviour

Your role with all the children in your placements is to:
- be fair
- be consistent
- understand which behaviour is appropriate for each age group
- have realistic expectations
- give brief explanations as to why you do not accept certain types of behaviour.

When children are cared for by more than one person, they will sometimes attempt to play one adult off against another. It is helpful, therefore, for both students and supervisors to follow the same approach. Consistency of care helps the child to know what is expected and acceptable. All children need to understand the limits set by their parents and carers as to what behaviour might be tolerated. As children grow older the rules may change but consistency is still the key for managing behaviour.

Behaviour is not acceptable if it:
- is dangerous, hurtful or offensive to someone else
- is dangerous to the child herself
- will make the child unwelcome or unacceptable to other people
- damages other people's property
- leads to bullying.

CASE STUDY

Mark, a second-year student, overhears a four-year-old child making a hurtful racist remark to a younger child.

1 What should be Mark's immediate reaction?
2 Should Mark discuss this with the supervisor?
3 What steps might the staff take to alter such behaviour?
4 How would Mark support the younger child?

The best way to manage unwanted behaviour is to:
- distract her or remove the child from the situation
- ignore swear words, as paying attention to them will make the child say them all the more
- say 'no', making sure your whole body shows that you mean it

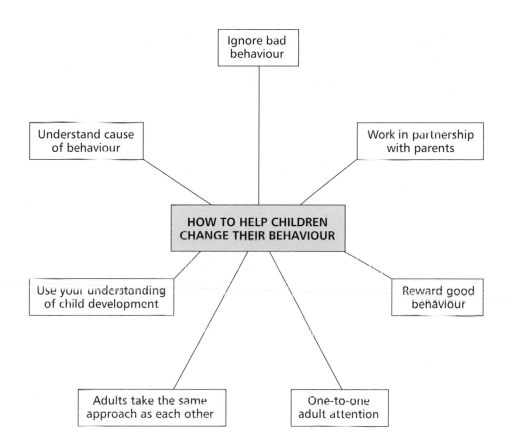

- refrain from rewarding unacceptable behaviour; that is, avoid giving the child your attention
- avoid arguing with a child in a tantrum
- show disapproval to make it clear that the behaviour is unacceptable
- make it clear that it is the *behaviour* that is not wanted, rather than the child
- explain why the behaviour is unacceptable if the child is old enough to understand
- resist smacking, shaking, biting or humiliating a child
- show affection and offer cuddles after an incident
- stay calm and in control of yourself.

When a child's behaviour causes concern, the question you need to ask is whether this is a normal stage in development, or a serious problem. Most problems sort themselves out in time, with the quarrelsome child becoming charming and manageable.

Activities

How might you manage the following situations?

1 An older child deliberately provoking his younger brother into losing his temper and throwing food on to the floor.
2 A three year old refusing to rest, although obviously very tired.
3 A three year old refusing to put on his coat to go outside in very cold weather.
4 A six year old taunting and teasing children from a different culture.
5 A child demanding sweets in a supermarket.

All the children in your placement, whatever their age, need your affection, consistency of care, understanding and an opportunity to play and learn. Bear in mind that children will copy adult's behaviour so you should make sure your behaviour sets a good example to the children. If there is a situation that you feel unable to deal with, you should immediately involve your supervisor.

11 CHILD PROTECTION

> **This chapter covers:**
> - **Definitions**
> - **Recognition**
> - **Procedures**
> - **Professional behaviour**
> - **Helping children to protect themselves**

These days, there is a great deal in the media about abused and neglected children and, while we must be careful not to over-protect children, we must always be alert to the dangers surrounding them. The whole of society has an obligation to protect children. The welfare of the child is always your first responsibility.

When in placement, if you have any concerns about a child, you must discuss this with your supervisor. If you feel that you are not being taken seriously, then you must talk to your tutor and ask him or her to follow it up.

The NSPCC estimate that 150–200 children die each year in England and Wales following incidents of abuse or neglect. Thousands more suffer emotional and psychological problems because of ill treatment by their parents or those looking after them. More than 20,000 children a year tell *ChildLine* they have been physically or sexually abused.

Definitions

Child abuse is sometimes difficult to define but you will need a clear understanding of the concept so that you can act with confidence when working with children. The broad categories of child abuse are: neglect; physical abuse and injury; and emotional abuse and sexual abuse. These categories can, however, overlap and interconnect. The following are some commonly accepted definitions of child abuse.

Physical abuse and injury: the intentional, non-accidental use of physical force and violence, resulting in the hurting, injuring or death of a child; this includes poisoning.

Physical neglect: the failure by the parent/carers to feed, shelter, keep safe, keep clean and provide medical care for a child.

Educational neglect: failing to meet the child's need for stimulation by not providing any opportunities for play and education to encourage language and cognitive development.

Emotional neglect: withdrawing or not providing love, affection and emotional consistency for the child, not providing an environment of warmth, interest and care.

Sexual abuse: 'The involvement of dependent, developmentally immature children and adolescents in sexual activities they do not fully comprehend, are unable to give informed consent to, and that violate the sexual taboos of family roles.' (Schecter and Roberge, 1976)

Emotional abuse: the exposure of children to constant criticism and hostility. It is always linked to emotional neglect.

Failure to thrive: the failure of a baby or child to achieve his or her expected weight or height with no obvious medical or physical cause. This is often associated with a negative relationship with the parent/carer.

Organized abuse: sexual abuse, and perhaps physical injury, with a number of perpetrators and a number of children. There is an element of deliberate planning.

Munchausen's Syndrome by proxy: a psychological condition, where the parent/carer fabricates a child's illness, seeking different medical opinions and inducing symptoms in the child to deceive the doctors, in order to gain the attention of medical practitioners.

Recognition

As a person who cares for children in a professional manner, you need to be able to recognize the signs of abuse and neglect. Your first duty is to the child, as laid down in The Children Act, 1989: 'the welfare of the child is paramount'. The following indicators should alert you:

- any bruises on the head or face of a small baby
- bruises on the cheeks of a toddler
- bald patches on the head
- cigarette burns
- two bruised eyes
- any neck injury
- 'fingertip bruising' (bruises the size of an adult's fingertips)
- bruises on genitalia
- adult bite marks
- scratches
- scalds on the child's feet and legs, caused by 'dunking' in very hot water
- splash burns
- babies unable to move any limb
- bruises on soft tissue
- injury to ear lobes
- bruising of lips, gums or a torn frenulum (the piece of tissue that attaches the lips to the gums).

SHAKING BABIES AND YOUNG CHILDREN

Shaking a child can cause serious injury, even death, yet many people are ignorant of the effects of such shaking. Shaking does not have to be done violently for it to cause serious damage. A baby who is shaken suffers similar damage to the brain as if it had been dropped on to concrete. A baby's head is large compared to the rest of the body and the neck muscles are not yet strong enough to support it. Shaking the head will cause tiny blood vessels to tear and bleed inside the brain. This can lead to loss of vision and hearing, fits, brain damage or death. Shaking can also cause serious harm to older children.

Signs to cause you concern would be a child arriving at your placement looking lethargic, with poor muscle tone, miserable, not interested in feeding and unable to settle. This may also indicate an onset of infection.

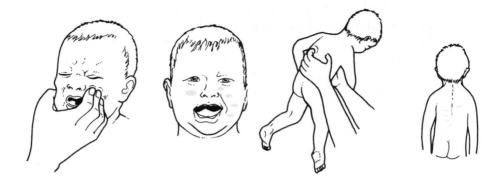

Fingertip bruising

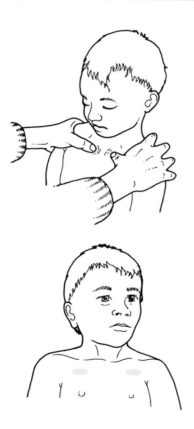

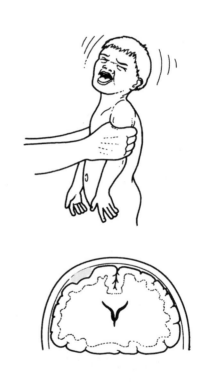

Thumb marks just below
the collar bone

Subdural haematoma caused by rapid
shaking of the head

Examples of fingertip bruising, thumb marks and shaking

Most children will suffer accidental injuries from time to time. Deciding what is accidental and what has been inflicted upon a child can be a very difficult process, testing the skills of experienced paediatricians. Many signs that might lead you to think that abuse has taken place might have another explanation entirely. For example, bald patches might occur if a child frequently pulls and twists the hair as a comfort habit.

Abuse and neglect may cause a change of behaviour that will vary a great deal according to the age of the child. You may see the child:

- withdraw from physical contact
- be wary of forming close relationships with adults and other children
- show apprehension when other children cry
- appear to be frightened of the parent/carer
- display a lack of spontaneity and become wary of adult's reactions to her
- display self-destructive behaviour such as hair pulling and head banging
- display aggression
- begin to over-eat or to refuse food
- fear new situations
- express comfort-seeking behaviour such as thumb-sucking, excessive masturbation and rocking to and fro.

The child may also show:

- speech disorders, such as stammering and stuttering
- delay in all-round development
- extremes of passivity and aggression
- low self-esteem and lack of confidence
- changes in sleep patterns and nightmares
- wetting and soiling after the child has become clean and dry
- temper tantrums which are not age-appropriate
- an inability to concentrate for more than a few minutes.

Changes in behaviour are not necessarily due to abuse or neglect. Children go through many difficult stages in their normal development. It is only when there is a *cluster* of behavioural changes that you should begin to consider the possibility of abuse.

CASE STUDY

Lyn, a second-year student, is concerned about Carrie, a small girl aged two years six months. She is behind in her developmental progress and is not gaining in weight and height as one would expect. She has been in day care for four months, and is the youngest of four children. Her mother is now a single parent, Carrie's father having left home shortly before her birth and made no contact since. She is often collected late, and by different people.

Carrie is not an easy child to look after in the group, always demanding attention and being very clingy with adults, especially Lyn. She is frightened of new situations. She enjoys her food, and eats well in the nursery, usually asking for second helpings.

1 Do you think there is cause for concern? Why?
2 What observations might help Lyn to find out more about Carrie's situation?
3 What records should the placement maintain for this child and her family?
4 How should Lyn respond to Carrie's clinging behaviour?
5 Are there any special activities Lyn might plan to help Carrie with her social behaviour?

SIGNS OF NEGLECT

A child who is underweight and possibly small for her age, with poor muscle tone and a dry wrinkled skin may be suffering from neglect. The child may arrive at the placement and immediately demand food, then display an enormous appetite during the day. If personal hygiene needs are not being met, the child may appear dirty and uncared for, smell of urine, have unbrushed hair and teeth, and wear inappropriate and dirty clothing.

A younger child may suffer from severe persistent nappy rash or cradle cap or both. She may appear constantly tired or lethargic, with frequent colds and coughs, stomach upsets and rashes, while the parents appear reluctant to seek any medical help. You may find the child frequently arrives and is collected late. You may notice that the parents fail to express any affection or display warmth and interest in the child, but seem to have unrealistic expectations of behaviour and capabilities. All these concerns must be discussed with your supervisor. It is unlikely, though possible, that your supervisor will ignore your concerns and be unwilling to take them further. This may be because the:

- relationship between your supervisor and the family is too familiar and he or she refuses to acknowledge that abuse could take place
- supervisor is too stressed and overworked to reflect clearly on the problem
- supervisor is unwilling to repeat a previous distressing experience
- supervisor feels that you are too inexperienced, and resents your interference.

CASE STUDY

Julian is three-and-a-half years old and has been attending Gina's nursery class placement for six months. The family is affluent, living in a large detached house. Julian's father is frequently away from home and Julian is usually collected from the class by an 'au pair'. The nursery has found it difficult to establish a relationship with Fay, Julian's mother. She seems to have very little time for or patience with Julian, often describing him in a disparaging manner. Julian is becoming more quiet and withdrawn and on one occasion describes being locked in a cupboard for what seemed to him to be all day. When his mother arrives to collect him one day she looks tearful and upset, and her hands are shaking. Julian runs and clings to his mother, who pushes him away. Gina is the only person to witness this incident.

1 What should Gina do?
2 How might his mother's rejection affect Julian's emotional development, and in what way would this threaten his later achievement at school?
3 What are Julian's needs, and what are the family's needs?
4 What might Gina and the nursery do to help Julian and his family?

Although very rare, you might find yourself in a placement where the practice verges on abusive behaviour. For example, where children are:
- made to sit at the table for long periods of time, and force fed
- handled roughly, their physical care needs delivered without concern for their dignity
- shouted at and made the brunt of sarcastic remarks.

For babies and toddlers in this type of placement, they may:
- not have their nappies changed frequently enough
- be left in their cots without stimulation for long periods of time
- be left to cry without being picked up.

If you feel worried about the practice in your placement or that your concerns about an individual child are not addressed, you must inform your tutor. As stated in The Children Act, 1989, 'the welfare of the child is paramount', so the tutors should support you in handling a very delicate and difficult situation.

It is very important that your behaviour and professional practice should be above reproach as you would not wish to find yourself in the position of being accused of abuse or neglect. The following chart will help you to protect yourself.

How to protect yourself from suspicion of child abuse in the placement

1 Do not show favouritism or spend too long with one child, unless it is following an observation and with the approval of your supervisor.

2 Do not take children to the lavatory by themselves until you have settled in and are aware of the policy of the placement.

3 Carry out intimate tasks for children only in the presence of other staff.

4 Do not arrange to see children or their families outside placement on any pretext. Do not agree to any babysitting arrangements.

5 Keep a daily log or diary to record your activities and movements.

6 Use only appropriate language in front of the children.

7 Be circumspect in how you approach children, do not touch or pick up a child who does not want to be touched or picked up.

8 Touches from children that worry you should be reported *at once* to your supervisor, as well as any other incidents that you feel uncomfortable about.

9 Do not ask children to keep secrets.

10 Managing children's challenging behaviour should never involve handling a child roughly.

11 Do not shout at or use a sarcastic approach with children.

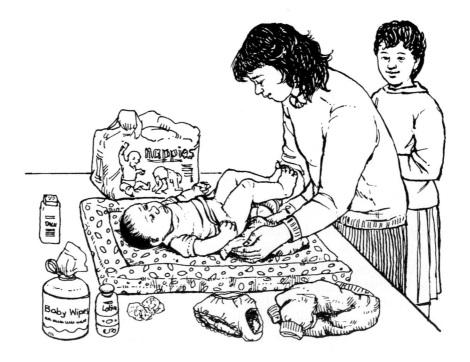

Procedures

Once suspected abuse has been recognized, certain procedures will be followed. It will depend on your particular placement how much you, as a student, will be involved and on your supervisor's assessment of your maturity and developing professional skills.

OBSERVATIONS

All child-care practitioners need to be meticulous and accurate in their record keeping. As a student who is regularly carrying out observations, you may be the one who first notices a child who is unhappy and who may be being abused or neglected. You would immediately discuss this with your supervisor. An up-to-date and frequent observation of a child who is suspected to be suffering from abuse is important evidence.

REFERRALS AND INVESTIGATIONS

Local authorities issue all establishments involved in caring and educating children with guidelines of the procedures to be followed in cases of suspected abuse or neglect. All establishments should have a child protection policy.

Activity
Ask your supervisor for a copy of the child protection policy for your establishment, along with access to the guidelines that they have been given by the local authority.
Then compare these with those obtained by other students in your group. Look for similarities and differences.

An investigation has to take place once abuse or neglect is suspected. The case will be referred to Social Services who will investigate the matter. A child protection conference may take place. Following this, a child may be placed on the register of children at risk; and a plan to protect the child, and help and support the family, will be drawn up.

Professional behaviour

It is difficult for an inexperienced person to deal with some of the issues that arise during a child abuse investigation. With the support of your supervisor and your tutor, along with your developing professional skills, you will face the challenge and learn a great deal from the experience.

CONFIDENTIALITY

If a child at your placement has been abused, and you are involved in any way, you will understand the necessity for strict confidentiality. Not only will you not discuss the case with any of your family and friends; you will also be trusted not to talk about it with other members of staff who are not part of the team dealing with it; nor with the families of other children in the placement. Some placements may feel that a case of child abuse is not something to be discussed with students and, if this is so, you must respect that view.

WORKING WITH PARENTS

There are many factors that might cause parents to abuse or neglect their children. Rarely are children taken away from their parents, so you might find yourself communicating with parents who have ill-treated their children. For the good of the children, you will need to maintain a professional relationship with these parents, however difficult you may find it.

Some children are abused by people other than their parents, such as close family members or trusted friends. These parents need a great deal of support and may approach you for advice. They may find you a sympathetic person and seek the opportunity to express their feelings to you. You will need to discuss with your supervisor the extent of your involvement and how appropriate this might be.

STRESS

Any reported case of an abused or neglected child is sure to arouse feelings of distress. This is even more stressful if you know the child and are involved in the protection process. You should inform your college tutor about what is happening in the placement, without breaking the rules of confidentiality. Your tutor should be able to advise you and support you during this time.

Helping children to protect themselves

Some of the children in your placement will come from families who are demonstrative and show affection by frequent kissing and cuddling. Other families, which may be equally fond of their children, may not be so outgoing with their emotions. You will need to build up a trusting relationship with each child and this will only happen with time. Children should feel they could always come to you for help and protection. It is important to involve the parents in helping children to protect themselves, as the message must be consistent.

When children are mature enough they should be told:

- the difference between comfortable and uncomfortable touches
- that safety rules apply to all adults and not just strangers
- that secrets they feel uncomfortable about should be discussed with a trusted adult
- any cuddles and kisses given by an adult 'in secret' should always be disclosed
- to feel good about themselves and know they are loved and valued
- to trust, recognize and accept their own feelings
- know that their bodies belong to them and nobody has the right to touch or hurt them
- that they can say no to requests that make them feel uncomfortable, even from a close relative or friend
- that they can rely on you to believe and protect them if they confide in you
- that they are not to blame if they are hurt
- that rules of good behaviour can be broken if they are in danger, and that it is perfectly all right to kick, bite, punch, scream and shout if they feel threatened
- that they must not speak to strangers however kindly they may appear, or go off with someone they do not know.

An organization, called 'Kidscape', was founded in 1984 to enable children to learn about personal safety and teach them strategies to keep themselves safe. It produces many useful leaflets and books. The NSPCC also produces a great deal of useful material.

GOOD PRACTICE IN CHILD PROTECTION AWARENESS

1 Read the placement child protection policy carefully, then ask your supervisor about any procedures you do not fully understand.
2 Observe children carefully but discuss any concerns you may have only with your supervisor or tutor.
3 Maintain the rules of confidentiality.

4 Treat all parents with respect.

5 Protect yourself from any accusations of abuse.

6 Do not make assumptions from very little evidence. Abuse is a very serious matter and you must not exaggerate what you have seen or heard.

7 Make sure you treat all children with respect and dignity, never shout or swear at or humiliate them.

You are unlikely to come across children who are abused or severely neglected during your training but if this should occur, we hope this chapter will support you and foster your awareness.

12 *PARENTS IN PLACEMENT*

> **This chapter covers:**
> - **Parents in placement**
> - **Different family types**
> - **Various child-rearing practices**
> - **Naming systems**

As you progress on your child-care and education course you will have realized how important it is to make good relationships with the parents of the children in your placement. The words 'parent' or 'parent/carer' are used to describe all primary carers, whether they are the child's biological parents, foster parents, adoptive parents, grandparents or others having responsibility for the child.

For some time it has been acknowledged that the support and hopes of parents play a vital part in the school life of the children. All the research shows the importance of parental involvement. Therefore parents need to

be kept well informed about their child's development and behaviour and understand how their children are taught.

Parents spend a great deal of time with their children and will know their strengths and weaknesses, be able to predict their needs and have made many decisions about their children in the early years. Therefore it is sensible to work with the parents for the benefit of the child. It will make the child more secure to see the parents and carer working together.

CASE STUDY

Pauline is in her late twenties and is a first-time mother. She has to return to work for financial reasons, so has settled her baby son of six months in a private day-care centre. He is well and happy and thriving but every morning Sarah, a second-year student, observes Pauline crying as she walks down the road to the bus stop.

1 How can Sarah help Pauline?
2 Should she discuss this with her supervisor?
3 Are there any outside organizations or professional workers that might be able to offer Pauline support?

Parents in placement

There are three main ways in which you may see parents being involved in their children's education and care establishments.

1 In management: parents are now on the governing bodies of schools and on the management committees of workplace and community nurseries. These parents will often be a visible presence in the schools or nurseries. In addition to discussing their own children, they will wish to be involved in general issues involving all the children and all aspects of provision. Parents have more power now than they have ever had.

2 In fundraising: through parent/teacher organizations or support groups, staff and parents working together often make good and useful relationships, not always connected with educational matters but nonetheless extremely valuable. The money raised usually goes towards improving the resources for the children.

3 Working with the children: this can range from helping with outings or swimming, to mixing paints and helping to clear up the room, through to involvement in daily routines such as helping at dinnertime. Some parents may be actively involved in the learning process, such as hearing children read or helping them to use a computer. Parental involvement can happen on a regular basis, for example being responsible for

a weekly cooking session; or sporadically, when help with a particular festival is required. It works most successfully when the parents know exactly what is required of them and have clear guidelines on how to carry out the activities. Encouraging parents to share in the planning of displays and special occasions can be rewarding and enhance both learning and enjoyment.

It is not possible for all parents to be involved, and establishments are usually sensitive about this. Some parents have full-time work, some have small babies to care for, and others may lack the confidence to take part. All parents who wish to be involved should be welcomed.

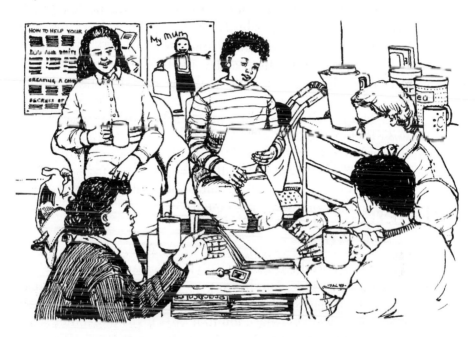

Activity
While working in your school placement, arrange to speak to the parent governor, with the permission of your supervisor, to find out more about this role.

Many establishments hold occasional workshops, often in the evening, for parents to work on aspects of the curriculum, perhaps making games, translating books, mending equipment or making mathematics more understandable. Some placements are fortunate enough to have a room set aside for the parents where they may learn a skill, take part in an activity or (for those for whom English is not their first language) become familiar with the English language. This is also a place for parents to socialize and make friends. In some larger schools there may be a crèche attached to allow the parents some time off from the youngest children, and some may run toy libraries.

You may be fortunate enough to accompany your supervisor on a visit to the home of a child who is about to be admitted to the placement. Not all placements have the staff cover to be able to carry out these visits. They can, however, be very useful for the family and the placement, as the home environment is a non-threatening place in which to discuss the child's needs.

Some day-care centres may run programmes to help parents understand the development and care needs of children. The parents can see how professionally trained people relate to their children and work alongside them.

As a student it may take some time for you to develop confidence in approaching parents and, indeed, it would be inappropriate for you to do so to discuss certain professional issues. However, in time you will need to become friendly and at ease with the parents of the children in your placement. When you greet a parent, smile and show you are approachable. Most parents/carers respond to a friendly and warm remark about their child.

If a parent approaches you and needs to talk, listen carefully and sympathetically. As a student, you will not be expected to give advice, but by being a good listener you will be valued and will have made a useful contribution to the work of the placement.

CASE STUDY

Jessie is in placement and feels that she is progressing well. She is upset and shocked when her supervisor asks her to wait after work and tells her that she has had some complaints from parents about Jessie's manner. They have found it difficult to talk to her, and complain that she is unfriendly.

1 Why might the parents have found Jessie unfriendly?
2 How can the supervisor help Jessie to make better relationships?
3 How can Jessie improve her body language?
4 Why is it important for Jessie to overcome this problem?
5 Might Jessie talk to someone else about this problem?

Different family types

It is important to understand the variety of families with whom you may be working in order to work in a positive way with all the families in the placement. These include the following:

The nuclear family: small family of parents and children, with no other family members living with them.

The extended family: family members outside of the parents and children, such as grandparents, aunts, uncles and cousins who may live with the family or close by, and who are in frequent contact with each other.

Lone parent family, sometimes known as single or one parent family: a mother or father plus children. Roughly 90 per cent of these households are headed by the mother, 10 per cent by the father. Of the women, the vast majority are divorced, separated from their partners or widowed.

Reconstituted family also known as merged or restructured family: parents have divorced or separated and re-married or are living with new partners and perhaps the partner's children.

Homosexual partnerships: two men or two women living together. The children may be brought into the family from previous heterosexual relationships, or adoption, or they have may have been born through artificial insemination by donor (AID), or via surrogacy. All the research carried out since the 1960s shows no differences in the social and emotional development of children living in these households, nor in their sexual orientation.

Other family types include groups of people living together and supporting each other, in a commune for instance, or within a community of travellers or Romanies. There are also some families who may be separated temporarily, while some members seek asylum from persecution and others may remain in the home country.

CASE STUDY

Ravi is a second-year student who has been contributing to the care of Rosie, aged two, in a day-care centre. He has established a good working relationship with Rosie's mother. For the last month, Rosie has been collected every Wednesday by her aunt. On the last two occasions, the aunt has been arriving very late, smelling of alcohol. Ravi knows that Rosie's mother, who is a lone parent, has to work late on a Wednesday.

1 How do you think Ravi should handle this?
2 What action might the supervisor take?
3 Describe any situations where an establishment might refuse to allow someone to collect a child.

Various child-rearing practices

Children's needs and parents' wishes may come from a cultural or religious source, arise from medical reasons or, quite simply, be an expression of what the parents want for their child. Parents' wishes and child-rearing practices must be respected and every effort made to comply with them.

There should be agreement and understanding about matters relating to:
- food, its preparation and eating, and any special diet
- personal hygiene
- skin and hair care, such as special creams and combs suitable for some African-Caribbean children
- the question of clothing during play, for example maintaining modesty in physical play, covering very curly or braided hair for sand play, or protecting the head and body against strong sunlight
- periods of rest and sleep, for example routines and comfort objects.

Do not assume that because a family is part of a particular cultural group, they necessarily follow all the practices of that culture. Some may observe all the customs of the group, whilst others pick and choose. To work in a positive way with all the families in the placement, it is important to understand the variety of cultures with which you may be working. However, the outward signs of a culture such as the way of dress, celebrating certain festivals and observing specific dietary laws, is not the whole story.

Janet Gonzalez-Mena points out in her book *Multicultural Issues in Childcare* (1993) that there are five areas in which students need to learn communication skills. There are many cultural differences in the concepts of smiling, eye-contact, sensitivity to personal space, touch and time. Each cultural group also shares certain child-rearing patterns and particular goals for their children. For example, many groups feel it is cruel to follow the Western custom of allowing babies to sleep on their own. Cultural groups are not immune to change. They can alter in response to the norms of the indigenous culture around them; attempts to 'educate' them to new ways; or to persuade them to accept indigenous definitions of 'women's rights'.

GOOD PRACTICE IN WORKING WITH PARENTS

1 Respect all parents as individuals and learn different ways of child-rearing from them.
2 Contribute to a welcoming and relaxed atmosphere, encourage parents to settle their children in and to spend time with them whenever they wish.
3 Avoid being patronizing with parents. Listen carefully to what parents tell you about their children and remember they are the experts on their own children.
4 Be professional at all times and never gossip about parents to other parents or within the team. If you should become aware of something that might affect the welfare of a child, go directly to your supervisor. Be careful not to jump to conclusions.
5 You may be at a placement near to where you live and so be familiar with some of the parents. You should discuss this with your supervisor as it might have a bearing on confidential matters.
6 A parent may wish to become very friendly with you and see you socially outside the placement. It is probably better to avoid this situation developing, as this may lead to ethical dilemmas and perhaps resentment from other members of the team.
7 When working with parents from other cultures who do not have English as a first language, try to learn a few words of their language (if only as a friendly gesture).
8 As a student you may be approached by parents seeking help with problems. These could be relatively simple or more complex, requiring outside professional advice. Remember that you will not be in the placement all the time, nor will you be there for very long, so a permanent member of staff should be involved in supporting any parent with concerns.

9 The quality of your observations will be much improved if you gain the permission and co-operation of the parents and occasionally share your notes with them.

10 You may be involved in having to deal with an angry parent. Listen to what is being said, keep calm, and do not respond angrily yourself. Seek the help of your supervisor to sort out the situation.

Naming systems

Many of the families in your placement may have names that, at first, appear to be similar. Take care, as some cultural and religious groups have different ways of naming their children.

Most Christian children have a first name, possibly a middle name and a surname in that order. It is important not to impose this on other groups of children, however, as this would be disrespectful.

African names will differ from one ethnic group to another: for example, in the Igbo language of Nigeria the first daughter will be called Ada, literally daughter. Other groups will name their children after the circumstances in which they were born, such as Mbita, born on a cold night. Traditionally, Africans do not have a family name, but most Africans in Britain will have adopted a surname that can be used for formal documentation.

The Chinese and Vietnamese communities use names in the reverse order; the family name is followed by the middle name and then the personal name. Children take the family name of their father. Some have now reversed the order of their name to follow the British pattern, so care should be taken when filling in records.

Muslim boys of Pakistani and Bangladeshi origin will often have a religious name before their personal names. Calling a boy Mohammed or Abdul, without adding the personal name, may well cause offence to observant Muslims. In the Middle East, however, Mohammed is itself a common personal name. Traditionally, there is no shared family name but, in order to conform with British naming patterns, some families might adopt a surname.

Many Muslim women have, in addition to their personal name, a title such as Begum, Bibi, or Nessa, which indicates that the person is female.

Sikhs place the personal name first. Singh is a common title, meaning lion, for men, as is Kaur, meaning Princess, for women. It would be inappropriate to address a Sikh woman as Miss or Mrs Singh or the father as Mr Kaur. In Britain, some Sikh parents give their children a first name and a surname only.

British Hindus place the personal name first. The Hindu surname is a shared family name indicating a family's traditional status and occupation.

If you are not sure how to address a child or a parent, ask your supervisor. You would not like to be referred to continually by the wrong name (for example, your surname only). Remember that many names have religious or cultural significance.

CHECKLIST

Have you:
- had the opportunity to be present at a home visit
- played a major role in settling a child and parent into the placement
- spoken regularly to most parents
- learnt a few words of another language
- involved parents in an observation
- worked alongside a parent in the classroom
- explained the value of an activity to a parent
- reached a better understanding of various ways of child rearing
- helped a parent with a simple problem
- met parents in a social setting within the placement
- been friendly and approachable to all the parents

- familiarized yourself with The Children Act, 1989, and the rights and responsibilities of a parent
- learned how to pronounce and spell the children's names correctly?

Activity
Make an information leaflet for parent/carers setting out how they might become involved in the nursery or classroom.

It is important to remember that your aim when working in partnership with parents, is on the education and protection of their child.

13 SUCCEEDING IN PLACEMENT

> ## This chapter covers:
> ■ **Professionalism**
> ■ **Anti-bias practice**
> ■ **Assessment in placement**
> ■ **Stress in the placement**
> ■ **Leaving your placement**

Your tutors and supervisors will be anxious for you to succeed in your placement and will be monitoring your professional progress as well as your developing skills in working with children. They will be assessing your increasing ability to put the theory you are learning into practice.

It is quite normal to feel stress if problems arise, and your tutors and supervisors are there to support you and help you with any difficulties.

Professionalism

Becoming a professional person is not something that happens overnight. With the help of tutors and supervisors you should regularly assess your knowledge, behaviour and attitudes. The professional person working with young children will have made progress in three areas: knowledge, behaviour and attitude.

KNOWLEDGE

During your course, both in the centre and in placement, you will be gaining knowledge. You will be learning about the physical, intellectual, language, emotional, and social development of children. This will make you sensitive to their needs and so help you to work well with children.

Knowledge plays an important part in preventative work, for example identifying children who are at risk of abuse and in need of protection. You will need to know the procedure for referral to make sure these children are safe. Although you may not be directly involved as a student, your supervisor will explain the procedures to you.

Acquiring knowledge never ends. A professional person is one who continues after qualifying to update him/herself regularly by attending courses, reading professional journals and always being ready to question and challenge in a thoughtful and constructive way.

BEHAVIOUR

During your placement, your motivation, enthusiasm and commitment will be continually assessed. You should show a positive attitude towards your work and become aware of your role and responsibilities. In this way, you will reach a clear understanding of what you can and cannot do in the placement. Good behaviour covers a number of areas that we shall look at one by one.

Attendance and punctuality

You must attend your placement regularly and be punctual. If you are unable to attend, or are unavoidably delayed, contact the placement so that they can replan the day. Keep them informed so that they know when to expect your return. At the end of your placement your supervisor will comment on your reliability and, in particular, your time keeping.

CASE STUDY

In her second term, Androulla missed a great deal of time in placement and in college. Her supervisor contacted the tutor, saying that when Androulla attended placement, she looked unwell and distressed but would not discuss it with anyone.

The next time Androulla was in college, her tutor spoke to her about her poor attendance. Androulla burst into tears and told her tutor that her father was in hospital, terminally ill, her grandmother had died, the family home had been burgled and her brother was on remand for a drug offence.

Her tutor organized some counselling and suggested that she took a term off.

1 How might this stress have affected Androulla's performance in placement?
2 What steps might she have taken to alleviate her distress?
3 Could she have tackled her problems in a more professional manner?
4 Which people might be able to help and support Androulla?

Communicating with others

How clearly you speak and the ways in which you talk to children, parents and other professional people will show them whether you are a caring,

knowledgeable, sensitive person, able to express your ideas clearly. Your body language should show that you are interested and motivated. Shrugging your shoulders and sulking is no substitute for expressing calmly and clearly your point of view over a disagreement. Maintaining eye-contact with children and adults will help good relationships.

Your ability to accept and act upon constructive feedback forms part of your professional development. When you are a qualified child-care and education practitioner, you will still need to look at and assess your work with others in the team, and be able to offer and accept suggestions for improvement.

Responsibility

The well-being and safety of the children in your care has to be your main priority, and at no time should you behave in a way that might put them at risk. No person is perfect in all respects, so understand and acknowledge your limitations. Do not feel forced to take on responsibilities when you feel that you have not had the necessary theory and training to carry them out successfully. If, for example, you are asked to assess children's reading and do not feel you have had enough experience, tell your supervisor that you are not ready to do this but would be willing to do something less demanding instead.

Confidentiality

Your placement will have on record much confidential information about the children and their families. The amount of information given to you will depend on what is necessary to meet the needs of the child, help you to work within the team and to gain deeper understanding of working with families. All information that you receive, whether written or spoken, is strictly confidential. You should never share it with your family and friends. Even your tutors will not want you to tell them the surnames of the children that you work with in your placement.

Working with parents

If you feel parents or carers want to confide in you, remind them that you are still a student; it may be more correct for them to discuss the problem with your supervisor or another member of staff. If they wish to talk only to you, ask their permission to give the information to the supervisor. If children confide in you, you must treat such confidences seriously, though you may well need to talk to your supervisor. Never promise children that you will not pass on information that they give you. Keeping quiet might mean leaving the child at risk, so the promise cannot be kept.

Activity

Make a list of other areas of work where people are called 'professionals'. Give reasons why they are called this.

CASE STUDY

Amelia, aged four, confides in Lauren, the student, that her mother is having a baby. Lauren is surprised as she knows that Amelia's father is in prison. When Amelia's mother arrives to take her home, Lauren congratulates her on her pregnancy in a loud voice. Amelia's mother looks very embarrassed. Lauren realizes that she has made a mistake.

1 What mistake has Lauren made?
2 How can she try to put it right?
3 Should she discuss it with the supervisor?

Attachment

Be careful about allowing children to become too attached to you. It is very flattering to have young children clinging to you but remember that you are only in placement for a short time, so cannot provide the continual comfort and care that is sometimes needed.

Opinions

If you have strong religious or political views, the placement is not the place to declare them. You may wish to raise some issues in the staffroom or at the centre, but it is unprofessional to do so in front of the children and their parents.

ATTITUDE

In your placement you will be expected to show an awareness and understanding of the total needs of all the children, parents and team members, regardless of race, class, culture, religion, disability, gender or age, both individually and in groups.

Never show favouritism or give special treatment to some children and not others. Always show respect and interest in the customs, values and beliefs of all the children with whom you are involved. This will help you to provide children with positive images of themselves and each other. Make it clear that you will not take part in gossip about children or their families.

Activity

With a group of friends, discuss how you would cope with a gossiping parent.

1 Would you tell your supervisor the gossip?
2 Could it be of benefit to the family being discussed?
3 If something serious is being talked about among the parents, such as abuse, should you keep quiet or pass it on to your supervisor, your tutor or anyone else?

Evaluating your performance on a regular basis, perhaps by keeping a diary, will allow you to become a reflective practitioner, one of the hallmarks of a professional.

Anti-bias practice

No member of society should be discriminated against because of his or her race, gender, class, culture, age, religion, disability or sexual orientation. This is especially important for those people working with young children. Children find it hard to challenge prejudice and need to feel confident about themselves and be sure that they are valued. If they do not feel good about themselves, they find it difficult to learn.

In your placement you may meet children from various backgrounds and cultures, with many different views of the world, possibly speaking different languages. There should be anti-bias policies available for you to read. The needs of children with disabilities to have access to equal opportunities is slowly being recognized and this should lead to all these children being included in all activities in the placement.

CASE STUDY

One of the parents asked a child-care student if there were any birthdays being celebrated that week. When Jayshree, the student, said that it was Andrew's birthday on Thursday, the parent said, 'Well, I won't bring Hannah in that day then.' On being asked why, the parent explained that the family were Jehovah's witnesses and that they did not believe in celebrating a special day for anyone.

1 How should Jayshree respond to the parent?
2 How do you think the placement should handle this in the short term?
3 What do you think should happen when there is another birthday?

Since The Children Act, 1989, anti-discriminatory practice is required by law in all establishments where there are children. The child's religion, racial origin, cultural and language background must be taken into account. This practice should help to promote positive images and give children confidence. Challenging prejudice is a major responsibility for all child-care and education practitioners.

GOOD PRACTICE IN ANTI-BIAS PRACTICE

1 Present positive images in your choice of books and use of equipment.
2 Present yourself as a good role model.
3 Admit what you do not know and be prepared to ask for help and advice.
4 Challenge all offensive remarks, whether from children or adults, against yourself or others.
5 Answer children's questions honestly, with explanations they can understand.
6 Make sure you pronounce and spell all the children's names correctly.
7 Make sure you know the names of the clothes the children wear.
8 Understand the different skin and hair care needs of all the children.
9 Encourage children to have positive feelings about their skin tone, hair texture and facial features.
10 Make sure you understand the importance of a varied diet, that will appeal to all the children and does not go against any cultural or religious taboos.

11 Challenge stereotypes. You may be watching a television programme with the children that shows girls in such a way that they appear inferior to boys. You will need to discuss this, pointing out that it does not depend on whether you are a boy or a girl as to whether you have the ability to be a leader, assertive, quiet or amenable.
12 Involve all children in all activities.
13 Encourage all children to be assertive and stand up for themselves.

FESTIVALS

There are a great many religious and cultural festivals celebrated all over the world. Quite a few of those celebrated in the UK have been 'adopted' from other cultures. We also join in the celebration of others, particularly those of the young children in our care, so the list can vary considerably.

Religious and cultural festivals

Autumn term	Spring term	Summer term
Harvest Festival	Rastafarian Christmas	May Day
Rosh Hashana (Jewish New Year)	Chinese New Year	Dragon Boat Festival
Yom Kippur (Day of Atonement)	Shrove Tuesday	Carnival
	Ash Wednesday	Raksha Bandhan (Festival of Sisters)
Sukkot (Jewish Harvest Festival)	Mothering Sunday	
	Passover	Father's Day
Ethiopian New Year (Rastafarian)	Ramadan	American Independence Day
	St Patrick's Day	
All Souls Day	St David's Day	Wesak
Divali (Festival of Light)	St George's Day	Pentacost
Guy Fawkes	Lent	Whitsuntide
Remembrance Sunday	Easter	Festival of Hungry Ghosts (Chinese)
Thanksgiving	Eid-ul Fitr	
St Andrew's Day	Saraswati Puja	Birthday of Haile Selassie
Birthday of Guru Nanak Dev Ji (Sikh)	Holi (Festival of Colour)	Birthday of Muhammad
	Baisakhi	
Chanukah (Jewish Festival of Light)	Martin Luther King Day	Janamashtarni
Advent	Lantern Festival (Chinese)	Shavuot
Christmas		World Environment Day
Kwanzaa	April Fool's Day	

It is important in our multicultural society, to know about festivals celebrated by all the ethnic and religious groups in the country, as well as the dominant Christian ones of Christmas and Easter and events such as Guy Fawkes and Halloween.

Children from all groups should feel that their culture and religion is respected by their peers. Groups of children drawn from just one culture should also have the opportunity to know about other cultures and understand that we live in a multicultural society. Where possible, parents should be involved in advising and organizing festival celebrations.

Activity
Look at the books in your placement. What percentage present positive images of race, gender, disability and various cultures?

Assessment in placement

The centre chooses the placements as suitable work models for students because they offer good practice in caring for and educating children. For this reason, it is your supervisor who will be responsible for assessing your progress, not only in your reliability and commitment but also in your growing awareness of what it means to be a team member.

PSR, PDPS AND PERS

Students on Certificate and Diploma level courses will be given a *Candidate Handbook* that will contain, in addition to general and assignment information:

- Placement Summary Record (PSR)
- Professional Development Profiles (PDPs)
- Practice Evidence Records (PERs).

Tutors will explain the importance of these forms. They have to be taken into each placement and completed by your supervisors. Care must be taken not to lose them, as they are part of your final assessment and will count towards your Certificate or Diploma.

Keep them carefully in a plastic folder. These profiles and records will be useful when you are being interviewed for a job, as they show in detail the skills you have achieved.

When the Placement Summary Record (PSR) is completed, you will find it useful to demonstrate to any potential employer the range of experience you have had in working with babies and young children. You will have a record of the names of the supervisors and the addresses of the placements that might be useful when you are seeking a reference.

VISIT BY TUTOR OR PLACEMENT ORGANIZER

The centre will arrange with your supervisor for you to be visited in your placement. The main reason for the visit will be to discuss your progress with both you and your supervisor. You may wish to talk about any problem you are having with your tutor first, so that he or she will help you to think about how you can raise this with your supervisor during the visit. This is part of your learning, as when qualified you will have to talk about difficulties with colleagues and try to sort out problems in a positive professional manner.

Often the use of a checklist aids a three-way discussion between student, tutor and supervisor by making sure that all good points are noted whilst showing where progress is needed.

If problems are identified and discussed openly, you should be able to state your point of view, and at the same time be prepared to accept fair, constructive criticism. At the end of the discussion it should be clear what you need to do to put right the problem and make progress. For example, a student who is constantly late will need to either get up earlier, or look again at the journey to the placement.

Tutor visit form

	Date of Visit	Name of Candidate		Name of Placement

	Unsatisfactory	Improving	Satisfactory
Professionalism:			
attendance			
punctuality			
knowledge of safety procedures			
Relationships:			
with children			
with team			
with parents			
Communication:			
speech			
listening skills			

Areas of strength

Areas for progress

Comments from candidate

Action plan

Candidate Signature

Supervisor Signature

Tutor Signature

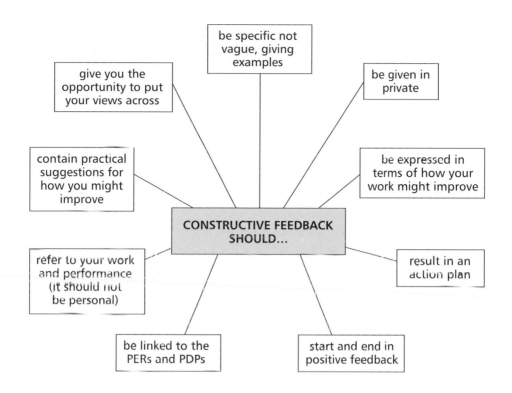

give you the opportunity to put your views across

be specific not vague, giving examples

be given in private

contain practical suggestions for how you might improve

CONSTRUCTIVE FEEDBACK SHOULD...

be expressed in terms of how your work might improve

refer to your work and performance (it should not be personal)

result in an action plan

be linked to the PERs and PDPs

start and end in positive feedback

Your performance in placement will show you whether you have chosen the right career and a course at the right level for you. If academic work is a struggle but the placement a joy, you are likely to succeed as you will be highly motivated to work very hard. If you find working with the children difficult and often boring, you will come to the conclusion yourself that you have made a wrong career choice. Your tutors will then guide you on to a more suitable course.

Stress in the placement

If you feel stressed, you must discuss it with your personal tutor, who should be prepared to look at the problem with you. Often a visit to the placement by the tutor and a discussion with you and the supervisor together can resolve the difficulty. Very occasionally, students do come to realize that they have made the wrong career choice and decide to change courses.

You may experience stress due to any of the following reasons:

1 You feel that you are asked to take on responsibilities and tasks that you are not prepared for.
2 There may be a conflict in the relationship between you and the supervisor.
3 You may not understand exactly what is required of you as a student and be unclear about the expectations of the centre and the supervisor.
4 You do not enjoy the work.
5 You may feel overwhelmed by the amount of work you have to complete in your placement.

Signs of stress may include one or more of the following:
■ a variation in appetite
■ insomnia
■ tiredness or lethargy
■ tearfulness
■ tension headaches
■ constipation or diarrhoea
■ high blood pressure
■ lack of concentration
■ inability to decide priorities
■ lack of interest in life
■ feelings of inadequacy
■ difficulty in making decisions
■ feeling neglected, overworked, tense and anxious
■ suppressing anger.

Someone who is stressed can often be ill and have to take time away from placement.

Coping with stress

You need to talk to your tutor, who should be able to advise you. You should also:

- learn how better to express your feelings and opinions
- manage your time more effectively, deciding what you want to achieve, the priority you give to each activity, and the time and energy you are prepared to devote to each activity
- look after yourself by eating a healthy diet, taking regular exercise, and avoid relying on nicotine, alcohol, caffeine or other drugs to keep you going
- talk about your feelings to others, and recognize your achievements
- remember the good, positive things that have happened rather than focusing on failures or difficulties
- have some time for yourself each day, when you are able to completely relax.

Activity

1 Identify and describe the areas of your working environment that you find stressful.
2 Consider ways in which you might limit this stress.

ASSERTIVENESS SKILLS

Learning to be assertive allows you to be open in expressing your feelings and needs. It encourages you to stand up for your rights and the rights of others. It has nothing to do with aggression. Instead, it is a technique that allows you to relate to others in an open and honest way, discussing problems and not personalities. Being assertive will enable you to:

- be more confident, decisive and comfortable in your role
- communicate better, as you will feel more able to express your views, identify problems and work with others to find solutions
- reduce levels of stress
- develop professionally and personally
- handle conflict, as you will be dealing better with difficult situations, where people are angry or upset.

As a student you may find yourself in a situation of conflict with other people in the team and even your supervisor. If you feel insulted, undervalued or ignored try to explain how you feel and why you feel that way.

Think about what you want to say, then discuss it first with a supportive friend. It is better to face up to situations rather than just hope they will sort themselves out on their own. Consider the other person's feelings and keep any discussion rational; do not allow it to become personal or insulting. Try to reach a suitable compromise so that no one will lose face.

COPING WITH VIOLENT BEHAVIOUR

You may be unfortunate enough to be in a situation where a parent behaves violently towards you or another team member. This is a rare occasion but if you feel threatened keep calm and do not respond in an aggressive manner. Maintain eye-contact but try and put some space between yourself and the parent. Do remember the safety of the children and staff comes first and report all incidents to your supervisor and tutor.

GOOD PRACTICE IN ASSERTIVENESS

1 Be natural. When asking for things or giving instructions, do not apologize or justify yourself. Ask politely, and keep it short and to the point.
2 Do not attempt to flatter or manipulate other people.
3 Accept it, when people say 'No', and do not take it personally.
4 If you say 'No', give a reason but do not apologize. Be calm and warm to show you are not angry or unhappy.
5 If you are interrupted, stay calm, and continue to speak until you have finished.

Being aware of the value of interpersonal skills is essential in child-care employment; and will be useful to you in all other areas of your life.

Leaving your placement

All good things come to an end. You may well feel sad at leaving a placement where you have been successful and made good relationships with staff and with children. Filling in the chart on page 171 might help you to assess your progress and prepare you for the next placement.

Make sure, in good time, that all your observations and activities linked to the placement have been completed, written up and signed by your supervisor. Remind your supervisor of your leaving date and request her to sign off the PERs and complete the PDP. Update the placement summary record in your *Candidate Handbook*.

Just before the day you leave, you should let the children know that you will not be returning to the placement as a student. If you say that you will come back to visit, you must be confident that you will be able to keep this promise. However fond you have become of the children, it is not professional to give full rein to your emotions as it may distress the children. Remember on the last day to say thank you to all the staff who have helped and supported you. Saying goodbye is not always easy but look forward to the next placement where hopefully you will make equally good relationships.

Self-assessment on completing placement

What I found most useful

_____

What I found most difficult

_____

What surprised me

_____

The skill/activity I most enjoyed was

_____

The skill/activity I least enjoyed was

_____

What I might have done differently

_____

In my next placement I will …

_____

Other comments

This form may be photocopied for student use. © Nelson Thornes

RESOURCES

Beaver, M. et al., *CACHE Level 3 in Child Care and Education*, Nelson Thornes, 2008

Brown, B., *Unlearning Discrimination in the Early Years*, Trentham Books, 1999

Dare, A. and O'Donovan, M.:
- *A Practical Guide to Working with Babies*, 4th Ed., Nelson Thornes, 2009
- *A Practical Guide to Child Nutrition*, 3rd Ed., Nelson Thornes, 2009
- *Good Practice in Caring for Young Children with Special Needs*, 3rd Ed., Nelson Thornes, 2009

Hobart, C. and Frankel, J.:
- *A Practical Guide to Activities for Young Children*, 4th Ed., Nelson Thornes, 2009
- *A Practical Guide to Child Observation and Assessment*, 2nd Ed., Nelson Thornes, 2009
- *Good Practice in Safeguarding Children*, 3rd Ed., Nelson Thornes, 2009

Malik, H., *A Practical Guide to Equal Opportunities 3rd Ed.*, Nelson Thornes, 2009

Nutbrown, C.:
- *Threads of Thinking: Young Children Learning and the Role of Early Education*, 3rd Ed., SAGE Ltd, 2006
- *Working with Babies and Children: From Birth to Three*, SAGE Ltd, 2008

Pound, L., *How Children Learn: From Montessori to Vygotsky – Educational Theories and Approaches Made Easy*, Step Forward Publishing Ltd, 2005

Silberg, J.:
- *Games to Play with Babies*, 3rd Ed., Brilliant Publications, 2004
- *Games to Play with Toddlers*, 2nd Ed., Brilliant Publications, 2005
- *Games to Play with Two-Year-Olds*, 2nd Ed., Brilliant Publications, 2002

Smidt, S., *A Guide to Early Years Practice*, 3rd Ed., Routledge, 2007

Tassoni, P. and Hucker, K., *Planning Play in the Early Years*, 2nd Ed., Heinemann, 2005

Walker, M., *A Practical Guide to Activities for Older Children*, 2nd Ed., Nelson Thornes, 2009

Child Education, Art and Craft and Infant Projects magazines, published by Scholastic Publications Ltd.

Nursery World magazine, published weekly.

INDEX

Page numbers in **bold** type represent charts, forms, worksheets and tables

abuse *see* child abuse
accident book   99–100
accidents   98–100
   prevention   **99**
activities   61–2
   anti-discriminatory practice   67
   equal opportunities   **65**, 66
   evaluation   **64**, 66–7
   health and safety   62
   safety   95
   supervision   95–6
activity plans   62–5, 66
After School Clubs   **13**, 24–5
agendas   73
aggressive behaviour   129
agreements *see* contracts
AIDS (Acquired Immune Deficiency
      Syndrome)   108–9
anaemia   117
anti-discriminatory practice   161–4
   activities   67
   cultural differences   **163**, 163–4
   curriculum plans   62
   and portfolios   60
appearance of student   27
asking children questions   75–6
assertiveness   169–70
assessment   164–7
   role of supervisor   164–5
attachment by children   160
attendance of student   158
attention-seeking behaviour   127–8,
      129
attitude of student   161

babies   15
   communicating with   74–9
   encouraging development   89–90
   play   82, 89–90
   safety   89–90, 95
   toys   89–90
balanced diets   110–12, **111**
behaviour   125–34
   due to abuse/neglect   139

influences on   127
   managing unwanted   132–3, **133**
   observing changes   55
   of student   158–61
benefits to placements   10
bilingual children   **77**, 77–8
body language   72–3
boredom   131
bottle feeds   112–14
Breakfast Clubs   **13**, 24
bullying   129

calories in food   110
Candidate Handbook   165, 170
care at home *see* family placements
challenging behaviour   127–30, **128**
   physical causes   129–30
checklists
   accidents   98–100
   children with disabilities   18–20
   family placements   15
   fire   98
   full-time day care   23
   hazards   100
   meeting with supervisor   32
   primary schools   18
   settling in   43
   speaking to children   75–7
   working with babies   15
   working with parents   155–6
   working with two to five year olds
      17
child abuse
   changes in behaviour   139
   confidentiality   144
   definitions   135–7
   investigations   143
   recognition of   137–9
   suspected   143
   working with parents   144
child-minders   **12**, 14
child neglect   136
   changes in behaviour   139
   signs of   140–1

suspected 143
child protection 135–46
    awareness 145–6
    Childcare Register 45
    policies 47
ChildLine 135
children
    communicating with 74–9
    helping them learn 93–7, **95**
    protecting themselves 145
Children Act (1989) 3, **4**, 141, 156
children at risk register 143
children with special needs *see* special
    needs
children's centres **13**
choosing child-care **25**
coeliac disease **117**
comfort behaviour 130
communes 152
communication **8**, 158–9
    with adults 68–74
community nurseries 13
completing placement 170–1, **171**
confidentiality 44, 59, 61, 160
    child abuse 144
consistency of care 132
constructive feedback 159, **167**
contracts
    between centre and placement 5
    between student and placement **33**
cost of child care **12–13**
Council for Awards in Children's Care
    and Education (CACHE) 62
cows' milk allergy **117**
crèches **13**, 24
criteria for placements 3–4, **4**
cultural differences **163**, 163–4
    eating 119–21, **120**
    naming systems 154–5
    working with parents 152–5
curiosity 131
curriculum 4, **12–13**
    see also National Curriculum
curriculum plans 62
cystic fibrosis **117**

daily activities of student 48–9, **49**
daily records 58–9, **60**
day care **13**, 20–3
day-care centres 20–1
day nurseries **13**
Department for Education and Skills
    (DfES) 82, 85

diabetes **117**
diaries 58–9, **60**
dietary customs **120**
diets 110–12, **111**
disabilities, children with 18–20
discussions with supervisor 32, 48,
    49
    activities 61, 95–6
    child protection 135
    observation notes 57
    signs of neglect 140

early learning goals 85
Early Years Foundation Stage 82–6
eating 122–3
    cultural factors 119–21
    emotional factors 118–19
    encouraging children 118–19, **119**
    healthy diets 110–12, **111**
educational neglect 136
emergencies, coping with 104, **104**,
    105
emotional abuse 136
emotional neglect 136
energy in food 110
environment of placement 32, 34
equal opportunities
    activities **65**, 67
    policies 47
    and portfolios 61
equipment (*Childcare Register*) 45
evaluation
    of activities 61, **64**, 66–7
    and portfolios 66–7
extended families 151

failure to thrive 136
family centres 13
family placements **12**, 14–15, 38–40
    first visit 28–30
    punctuality 38
    what placement might offer **40**
    what student might offer **39**
family types 150–2
favouritism 142, 161
fee-paying schools 18
feedback, constructive 159, **167**
feeding babies 112–16
festivals, religious/cultural **163**,
    163–4
finger foods 116
first aid 6, 99, 104
first visit

family placements   28–30
   group care   31–2
food
   healthy diets   110–12, **111**
   policies   47
food hygiene   **121**, 121–2
food poisoning   122
food refusal   123, **123**
formal meetings   73–4
formula milk   112–13
full-time day care   13, 20–1

German measles   108
'grazing'   124
group care   40–4
   first visit   31–2
   settling in   40–1, 43–4
   student responsibilities   **42**
   working in a team   41, 43, 50
group dynamics   41

handling babies/children   74–5
hazards   100
Health and Safety at Work Act (1974)
   98
health and safety
   activities   62
   legislation   3
   policies   47
health
   personal   105–8
healthy diets   110 12, **111**
healthy eating habits, encouraging
   124
hidden agendas   41
HIV (Human Immunodeficiency
   Virus)   108–9
holiday play schemes   **13**, 21
home placements *see* family placements
homosexual partnerships   151
hospitals   26
hygiene
   food   **121**, 121–2
   personal   107–8, 109, 121

illness of student   50
independent schools   18
induction   **37**, 37–8
infant schools   **13**
   activity plans   63
infection   105, **106**
inspection of placements   3, **12–13**

jealousy   128

Key Stages   87–8
key workers   20, 23, 91
Kidscape   145
knowledge acquisition   157–8

labelling children's work   69, **70**
learning goals   62, 63, 66, 85
leaving placement   170 1, **171**
listening skills   72
logs   58, 59, **60**, 142
lone parent families   151

mealtimes   116, 122–3
medicines, storage   100
meetings
   with adults   73–4
   formal   73–4
   with supervisor   32, 49
   see also discussions with
      supervisor
memoranda (memos)   68–9
minutes of meetings   73
mobiles   89
Multicultural Issues in Childcare   153
Munchausen's Syndrome by proxy
   136–7

naming systems   154–5
nannies   **12**, 14
National Curriculum   5, 18, 63, 82,
   86–8
neglect *see* child neglect
normal development   54
NSPCC   135, 145
nuclear families   151
nursery chains   20
nursery classes   **12**, 16
nursery schools   12, 15–16
nursery teachers   15, 16

obesity   **117**
observations   55–6
   changes in behaviour   56
   children's needs   57
   identifying good practice   56–7
   methods   57–8
obstetric wards   26
Ofsted   3, 4, **12–13**, 14, 44–7, 82,
   83
one parent families   151
opinions of student   161

organized abuse 136
out-of-school care **13**, 24–5

paediatric wards 26
parent workshops 149
parents as partners *see* working with parents
passive smoking 102
personal hygiene 107–8, 109, 121
physical abuse/injury 135
physical neglect 135
Placement Summary Record (PSR) 165
placement types **11–13**
placement worksheet **35**
placements **1**
   abusive behaviour by 141
   difficulties with 36
planned play experiences 4
play 82
   babies 89–91
   toddlers 91–3
play equipment, toddlers 91
playgroups **13**, 23–4
policies and procedures 47–8, 49
portfolios 55, 59, 62
   anonymity of children 61
   anti-discriminatory practice 61
   equal opportunities 61
   evaluation 66–7
   safety and protection of children 61
Practical Guide to Activities for Young Children, A 89
Practical Guide to Child Nutrition, A 110
practical skills of student 5–7
Practice Evidence Records (PERs) 165
pre-schools **13**, 23–4
premises (*Childcare Register*) 45
preparation for placement 27–8, **29**
primary schools 17–18
private infant schools **13**
private nursery schools **12**
Professional Development Profiles (PDPs) 165
professionalism **9**, 59, 61, 144, 157–61
punctuality 38, 50, 158

reading
   to children 79–81
reconstituted families 151
records (*Childcare Register*) 45
referrals 55
refusing food 123, **123**
registered person (*Childcare Register*) 46
registration certificates 3
registration of Settings 44–7
religion and diet **120**
religious differences *see* cultural differences
resources, production of 63
responsibilities, student **42**, 159
routines 66
rubella 108

safe environments 102, 104
safety 61, 98–105
   activities 96
   babies 89–91, 95
   Childcare Register 45
   toddlers 91–3, 95
safety labels **103**
safety standards 101
salt in diet 112
school-based placements 14–20
self-assessment **6, 171**
self-development **7**
self-evaluation 161
sessional day care **13**, 23–4
settling in
   difficulties 54
   group care 40–1, 43–4
sexual abuse 136
shaking babies/children 137–8
singing to babies 90
single parent families 151
snacks 112
solid food 114–16, **115**
speaking
   to adults 68
   to children 74–8
Special Care Baby Units 26
special diets 116–18
   common disorders **117**
special needs 19–20
   curriculum plans 62
special schools **13**, 18–20
staff qualifications **12–13**
   day-care centres 20
   family placements 14

pre-schools   23–4
staffing
  community nurseries   **13**, 148
  day-care centres   20
  nursery classes   16
  nursery schools   15–16
  pre-schools   23–4
staffing ratios   **12–13**
staffrooms   43, 48, 50
state infant schools   **13**
state nursery schools   **12**
stereotyping   127, 163
sterilization of bottles   114
stress   168–9
sugar in diet   112
suitable person, *Childcare Register*   45
summer camps   **13**
supervision of activities   95
supervisor role   34–6, 67
  assessment   164–5
  meetings   32, 49
  see also discussions with supervisor
suspicion of child abuse   **142**
swearing   77

teamwork   41, 43, 50
telephone use   71
temper tantrums   127–8

toddlers
  outings   91
  play   91–2
  play equipment/toys   91–2
  safety   92–3, 95
  walking   91–2
toilet-training   6, 91
toys
  babies   89–90
  toddlers   91–2, 95
traveller families   151–2
treasure baskets   90
tutor visits   165–8, **166**, **167**
types of placement   **11–13**

weaning   114–16, **115**
withdrawn behaviour   129
work experience placements   **2**, 5
working in a team   41, 43, 50
working with parents   147–50, 153–4, 160
  cultural differences   152–5
  Childcare Register   45
  parents' wishes   152
  policies   47–8
  violent behaviour   170
workplace nurseries   **13**, 21
writing skills   69–71

NOTES ON OBSERVATIONS

NOTES ON ACTIVITIES

MEETINGS WITH SUPERVISORS

WEEKLY TIMETABLE